BEGINNING
THE
PRINCIPALSHIP
THIRD EDITION

To Bridget and Stephanie
and the many educational leaders
who served as the inspiration for
helping readers begin the principalship

JOHN C. DARESH

BEGINNING THE PRINCIPALSHIP

A PRACTICAL GUIDE FOR NEW SCHOOL LEADERS

THIRD EDITION

FOREWORD BY
VINCENT FERRANDINO,
Executive Director, National Association of Elementary School Principals
and GERALD N. TIROZZI,
Executive Director, National Association of Secondary School Principals

A Joint Publication

CORWIN PRESS
A SAGE Publications Company
Thousand Oaks, California

NAESP
NATIONAL ASSOCIATION OF ELEMENTARY SCHOOL PRINCIPALS
Serving All Elementary and Middle Level Principals

NATIONAL ASSOCIATION
OF SECONDARY SCHOOL
PRINCIPALS

For information:

Corwin Press
A Sage Publications Company
2455 Teller Road
Thousand Oaks, California 91320
www.corwinpress.com

Sage Publications Ltd.
1 Oliver's Yard
55 City Road
London EC1Y 1SP
United Kingdom

Sage Publications India Pvt. Ltd.
B-42, Panchsheel Enclave
Post Box 4109
New Delhi 110 017 India

Printed in the United States of America

10 09 08   5 4 3 2

Library of Congress Cataloging-in-Publication Data

Daresh, John C.
Beginning the principalship : a practical guide for new school
leaders / John C. Daresh.— 3rd ed.
    p. cm.
Includes bibliographical references.
ISBN 978-1–4129–2681–2 (cloth) — ISBN 978-1–4129–2682–9 (pbk.)
    1. First year school principals—United States. 2. School management and
organization—United States. 3. Educational leadership—United States. I. Title.
LB2831.92D37 2006
371.2'012—dc22

                                            2005031776

Acquiring Editor:	Elizabeth Brenkus
Editorial Assistant:	Desirée Enayati
Copy Editor:	Diana Breti
Typesetter:	C&M Digitals (P) Ltd.
Proofreader:	Doris Hus
Cover Designer:	Michael Dubowe

Contents

Foreword

What a pleasure to join our sister organization, the National Association of Secondary School Principals, in support of this foundational book. Within these pages, John Daresh shares with aspiring and new principals sage advice on and strategies for effectively leading the schools of our nation. I found many scenarios and examples within to ring true as to the kinds of challenges and joys this important job brings. The demands on the principal are many; however, the opportunities to inspire and reach every child are also great. This book will help paint a picture of the principal as a full person, helping new school leaders hone the technical and managerial skills, leadership practices, relationship skills, and personal intentions that are all a special part of the job. Great schools reflect great principals, and this book will help new leaders on their way!

—Vincent Ferrandino, PhD
Executive Director, National Association
of Elementary School Principals

John Daresh's depiction of the principalship stays grounded in the day-to-day realities of the school leader's professional life, yet retains a focus on the priority of the teaching and learning process—a lesson that I hope will guide all of your professional decisions, and one you will surely revisit as you continue to develop as a leader. As No Child Left Behind shifts the focus to school-level success, the need for a guide in beginning the principalship is greater than ever before. If you're a new principal reading this book, I welcome you to what could be the most challenging and rewarding position you'll ever have; and I commend you for recognizing the value in learning all you can about the important job you're assuming.

—Gerald N. Tirozzi, PhD
Executive Director, National Association
of Secondary School Principals

Preface

In the 1980s and 1990s, predictions were made that school districts across the nation would face a shortage of principals in a very short time. Those predictions have come true. It is not uncommon to hear of situations where large school districts are facing the need to hire 20% or more new principals each year for the foreseeable future. It is truly a great time to think about pursuing a career in the principal's office.

But many educators do not want the opportunity to serve as school leaders. Staying in the classroom is a tempting choice for many who think of the principalship as becoming an increasingly "undoable" job. After all, finding money to operate schools is tougher than ever before. Accountability mandates are making the job of principal one filled with constant challenges to ensure that state test results are acceptable. Afterschool activities never seem to decrease, to the extent that many principals speak jokingly about "8-day work weeks, with 25 hours of duty each day."

Despite all the limitations to the principalship as a job, there are other realities. For one thing, principals often note that their jobs are the best things they have done in long careers in education. And above all, there is great satisfaction in seeing students learn each day, often as a result of efforts made by the principals to improve schools "from the inside out."

Nothing will ever make the job of being a principal easy. But what is suggested in this book is meant to give a beginning principal some degree of hope that the work is a calling worth answering. Great things will happen, and we hope that some of the ideas will help you succeed and not just survive.

Several changes have been made in this third edition. Four new chapters have been added. Chapter 6 looks at the ways in which a beginning principal needs to be able to meet the expectations of the community in addressing mandates for more accountable schools. Chapter 7 describes the ways in which a new campus leader must be sensitive to working with all who serve the children in a school. Too often, we think only about classroom teachers and some additional professional staff such as the school nurse, counselors, or site-based social workers or school psychologists. Many people are involved with assisting students in their learning.

Chapter 8 includes some suggestions for working more effectively with parents of the students in your school, and finally, Chapter 15 has been added to give you a few general tips shared by some very wonderful people who are also great colleagues. Despite all the challenges of being an effective principal, never stop having fun with your assignment.

Acknowledgments

One cannot write a book that describes the ways in which someone can begin the school principalship with an attitude of optimism unless there are a lot of people who also believe in the ways in which leaders can touch the lives of young people and encourage great futures. There are a lot of people who share my dream that we can ensure great things in the future of schools by continuing to support those who accept the challenges of service as a school principal. Among these are my colleagues that I have met and worked with in the field. People like Jim Kelch, Debbie Livingston, Nick Cobos, Armando Aguirre, Mary Beth Cunat, Nancy Laho, Ron and Maureen Areglado, Carolyn Grantham, Bobby Ortega, and many other school leaders across the nation serve as living reminders of what great schools can be with great leadership. And my university colleagues also dedicate themselves to the values of preparing effective school leaders for the future. Among these valued friends and colleagues are people like Rick Sorenson, Rodolfo Rincones, Phil Kramer, Arturo Pacheco, Bruce Barnett, Gene Hall, Kathy Whitaker, Myrna Gantner, Dick King, and many others who continue to work toward better schools by preparing great school leaders.

Finally, I again note my appreciation for my friends and colleagues at Corwin Press. Gracia Alkema started this project, then Robb Clouse and Douglas Rife supported a second edition. Now the project continues with Lizzie Brenkus as my new leader.

Corwin Press gratefully acknowledges the contributions of the following individuals:

Jim Hoogheem
Principal
Fernbrook Elementary School
Maple Grove, MN

Randy Shuttera
Assistant Principal
Neptune Middle School
Kissimmee, FL

Stephen Handley
Principal
Terry High School
Terry, MS

Kevin Fitzgerald
Principal
Caesar Rodney High School
Camden, DE

About the Author

 **John C. Daresh** is a professor of educational leadership at the University of Texas at El Paso. Over the years, he has held faculty or administrative appointments at the University of Cincinnati, The Ohio State University, and the University of Northern Colorado. He has worked as a consultant for universities, state departments of education, and school districts across the United States, and also in Canada, France, Holland, Israel, the United Kingdom, South Africa, and Taiwan. In addition to his university appointment, he serves the Chicago Public Schools as the lead consultant on principal mentoring, a central part of the district's strong commitment to the creation of more effective instructional leaders to serve the children of the nation's second largest school system.

Introduction

Mark Carlisle was an elementary school teacher for 11 years when he decided that he wanted to leave the classroom and pursue a career as a school administrator. He knew that by following that path he would be leaving his students and many of the things that he enjoyed about his profession, but he saw administration as a way to help serve more students. He knew he was a good teacher, but he wanted some new challenges. As a result, he began taking graduate courses at Mountain State University with the expectation that he would soon qualify for a state principal's certificate, a necessary first step toward his goal of becoming an elementary school principal.

Mark completed his master's degree in educational administration at Mountain State, and then he passed the state administrator certification examination and received his principal's certificate. He applied for and received his first administrative position in his school district. He was assigned to serve as assistant principal at Baker Middle School where he worked with Frank Thomas, one of the most respected and experienced principals in the county. After three years, Mark and Frank believed that the young assistant was ready to apply for one of the elementary school principalships that were open in the district.

Mark's dream of a principalship became a reality last spring. He was hired as principal of Guilder Green Elementary School, the smallest and oldest building in the school district. It is now October, six weeks into his first school year as a principal. Mark remains convinced that going into administration has been a good career move, but there are times when the excitement and enthusiasm he felt when he was first offered the job begin to fade. Sometimes he wonders whether he would rather be an assistant or even go back to the "good old days" as an elementary school teacher.

Mark has found that life as a principal is quite a bit different than it was as an assistant. For one thing, at his current school he has no assistant; he's on his own as the sole administrator. Also, he remembers the words of his mentor, Frank Thomas, and now he appreciates that Frank was truly in the "hottest seat" in school. Frank used to tell him that assistants only get the "warm seat." He knows that the "buck" truly does stop on the principal's desk.

He has now discovered that one of the most frustrating things about the principalship is not that he can't handle the job of managing his school. He has an excellent secretary and a very talented and experienced teaching staff, and he feels he learned some very practical skills during his time as an assistant principal and also during the internship that he completed a few years ago as part of his training at Mountain State. What he is really beginning to feel is that life as a principal is emotionally draining. He knew that there would be conflict as an administrator. He learned that lesson during his time as an assistant principal when he quickly appreciated the fact that "administrators are not paid to win popularity contests." As the principal (and sole administrator in the school), he is now truly surprised at the number of personnel issues he has to deal with each day. On top of that, he suddenly has recognized how lonely he is beginning to feel in his office. As an assistant, he met with the principal almost every day for at least a few minutes. Now he is on his own. Dr. Pringle, the superintendent of schools, has dropped in on Mark a couple of times this fall. The other elementary principals with whom Mark meets on the third Thursday of every month are all friendly enough, but they are too busy to do much more than say hello to Mark when they see him. If they get together for lunch before heading back to their campuses, they never want to talk shop.

All of this makes Mark Carlisle feel very much like a real rookie who has no connection to anyone or anything.

National surveys conducted by the National Association of Elementary School Principals (NAESP) and the National Association of Secondary School Principals (NASSP), and also research carried out by state administrator associations and state educational agencies, has shown that within the next few years more than half the principals in the United States (and in many other countries around the world) will be able to retire and leave the school principalship if they so desire. Also, there is a steady rise in the school-age population of many areas in this country. As a result of these factors, more and more people will be going into school principalships for the first time.

At the same time that we will see more rookie principals, however, we will also see rapid changes in society. As a result, students are changing drastically, political pressures on schools are increasing, and public expectations for performance by schools are mounting; the business of running schools is different from what it was just a few years ago. The principalship has never been an easy job. The last few years have made the job even more demanding and difficult.

On the basis of your experience as a teacher or assistant principal, list some of the ways in which changes in your community, school district, or students have drastically altered your role as a professional educator (for example, perhaps many new students for whom English is not their primary language have been moving into your school district).

_____

_____

_____

_____

If you are not currently a principal, you can imagine how the issues listed above have made the life of a school principal today different from what it was only a few years ago. If you are a principal, you probably already know that these issues significantly affect your work each day.

The effect that all these changes in society have had on the work of school leaders is profound. As a consequence, traditional patterns of accommodating newcomers to principalships are less acceptable. In the past, it was often possible for the superintendent to hand the school keys to the new principal and simply advise, "You're the boss now. Try not to foul things up too badly this first year. Learn on the job from those who have more experience." Such haphazard approaches to supporting educational leaders first coming on board are not consistent with the increased expectations and demands by parents, legislators, and other community members that schools become more productive, accountable, and effective. There is much less wiggle room for new principals than ever before. Rookies must now step aboard and perform with the same skill and effectiveness as colleagues who have been in leadership roles for many years.

The beginning principal today often faces a work environment in which there is little or no tolerance for those who might make mistakes. State mandates and federal legislation such as the No Child Left Behind Act define much of what school principals are supposed to do. Central office administrators and local school board members are much less tolerant of errors and poor performance than ever before. And because school administrators now face the same pressures for "perfect performance," beginning principals are not always able to have supportive relationships with their more experienced colleagues.

This book does not pretend to offer magic recipes to be followed by beginning principals. There will not be a simple list of 10 or 11 ideas that will always lead you to success. However, I will share insights derived from the experiences of many successful educators and also from extensive research on the needs of beginning school principals. A lot has been learned about the kinds of things that might help Mark Carlisle and you as you proceed through the opening stages of your administrative career in schools. One of the most important things discovered over the years is that from the start of your life as a school leader, you can always look at your new job in two very different, often competing, ways:

- How to survive the principalship
- How to be an educational leader

These two ideas are certainly not mutually exclusive. As many school administrators point out, you cannot become a leader if you do not survive your first few days in the principalship. But there are many people who look to the challenges of the principalship only in terms of making it through from one day to the next. They tend to think only in terms of short-term skills—how to stay out of trouble or how not to get fired.

In the chapters that follow, you will certainly learn some of the kinds of things that will help you keep your job. However, simple survivorship will be only part of what you will learn. The legacy you will share here is that of leadership development— how even the greenest rookie can position himself or herself so that more effective school practice will result. If this stance were not taken, there would be no support here for the best practices of school principals. After all, effective principals will lead effective schools, and effective schools are what all educators are interested in developing and maintaining.

PLAN FOR THE BOOK

Throughout this book, I will review many of the issues and concerns that are faced by beginning principals. These concerns are described through a conceptual framework developed and explained in Chapter 2. A statement of some of the problems faced by beginners and some strategies you might wish to follow in dealing with these problems is included.

Later chapters will explore other aspects of life as a new principal, and each chapter looks at one or more of the major issues faced by beginning school principals. A major addition in this edition is a consideration of the ways in which a beginning principal might be able to face the expectations of state and federal accountability standards. Chapter 6 considers the ways in which an effective principal, whether a beginner or a more seasoned veteran, can improve a school by involving groups not traditionally viewed as part of the formal educational community as partners in educational improvement. Chapter 13 discusses the value of developing a clear educational platform, or statement of professional values, to guide your work. This is one method of helping you develop greater self-awareness as you assume your new professional role.

An important part of each chapter will be a concluding section in which you are invited to develop a personal plan for improvement and professional development that is consistent with the issues described in that chapter. Through this technique, you will be able to create a professional portfolio and personal growth plan that may help you reflect on your first years as a principal. More and more school systems and states are demanding that administrative personnel create portfolios as a way to guide their personal and professional development. Portfolios assist educators to become more focused on their career needs, but in many cases, they become little more than scrapbooks that include a lot of random, disconnected artifacts. Using your responses in the personal plan sections throughout the book, you can create a portfolio that will lead you through the next important steps in your career.

SUGGESTED READING

Alvy, H. B., & Robbins, P. (1998). *If I only knew . . . Success strategies for navigating the principalship.* Thousand Oaks, CA: Corwin Press.

Belker, H. B. (1993). *The first-time manager* (3rd ed.) New York: American Management Association.

Blaydes, J. (2004). *Survival skills for the principalship.* Thousand Oaks, CA: Corwin Press.

Brock, B. L., & Grady, M. L. (2004). *Launching your first principalship: A guide for beginning principals.* Thousand Oaks, CA: Corwin Press.

Carr, C. (1995). *The new manager's survival manual* (2nd ed.). New York: John Wiley.

Chapman, E. N. (1992). *The new supervisor* (Rev. ed.). Los Altos, CA: Crisp Publications.

Daresh, J. C. (2002). *What it means to be a principal.* Thousand Oaks, CA: Corwin Press.

Dunklee, D. R. (1999). *You sound taller on the telephone: A practitioner's view of the principalship.* Thousand Oaks, CA: Corwin Press.

Hart, A. W. (1993). *Principal succession: Establishing leadership in schools.* Albany, NY: SUNY Press.

Hill, L. A. (1992). *Becoming a manager: How new managers master the challenges of leadership.* New York: Penguin Press.

Pedler, M., & Boydell, T. (1985). *Managing yourself.* London: Fontana Press.

Straub, J. T. (2000). *The rookie manager: A guide to surviving your first year in management.* New York: Amacom.

Wilmore, E. L. (2002). *Principal leadership: Applying the new Educational Leadership Constituent Council (ELCC) standards.* Thousand Oaks, CA: Corwin Press.

2

A Framework for Understanding the Beginning Principalship

Fewer than 20 years ago, concerns of beginning principals were not really considered important by educational researchers. The truth of that statement is readily apparent if you take time to glance at the literature on educational administration over the past 75 years. Many books and articles focus on the role of the principal, of course. We know a lot about the duties of principals, the kinds of conceptual and practical skills that must be demonstrated, and we even have excellent descriptions of what the life of a typical school principal is like. Harry Wolcott's (1973) study, *The Man in the Principal's Office: An Ethnography*, remains what many describe as the best analysis of what building administrators (men and women) do on a daily basis.

Because of a recognition of the critical need for new people to move into principalships across the United States, however, there has been an equivalent understanding that research on the world of novice administrators would not only be interesting but important as a way to inform the development of policies and practice. This chapter looks at research on the work of beginning principals and uses this analysis to establish a method by which you can compare the kinds of issues that you are facing with what other principals faced when they first came on board.

CASE STUDY: FIGURING OUT THE PAPERS

Maricela Chavez was in her first two weeks of her first principalship of an elementary school in the Northern City Public Schools. She had eight years of experience in the classroom as a teacher and then four years as a central office coordinator for special education programs in the southwest region of the city. While she was coordinator, she worked on her master's degree in school administration and received her certificate as a principal. She was fortunate to get a call to serve as the principal of the John M. Smythe Elementary School on the south side soon after she applied last spring.

When the superintendent offered her the job, he told Maricela that although she was his selection to be the new principal at John M. Smythe, she still had to be appointed by the district school board at its monthly meeting in June. As expected, the board approval was merely a formality. She was introduced to the public as the new principal of the small but well-respected school. The next day, she proudly went to the central office to get her keys, policy manual, and all other assorted paraphernalia, mail, and notes left by the previous principal. She skimmed over the mound of paper in front of her and suddenly began to get a bit uneasy about her new job. From her previous experience as an assistant principal, she knew that a big part of the principal's job would involve keeping detailed records and filling out forms, but she was already nearly overwhelmed by the procedures required for working on many of the district forms, completing state department of education report sheets, and responding to the never-ending supply of memos, correspondence, and other paperwork that filled her incoming mail basket. She had a lot of similar work to do as a teacher, special education coordinator, and assistant principal, and she was aware that her principal for the last four years always seemed to be filling out forms, but all of her past experience seemed minimal now that she was sitting in the real "hot seat" of the principal.

CASE STUDY: TO GO OR NOT TO GO

Dan Carter was very happy to become an elementary school principal in the Hightower Independent School District. For the past two years, while he completed university courses leading to administrative certification, he had looked forward to landing a job as a principal some day. The night in June when the Board of Education approved his appointment was a great time for Dan and his family. Everyone came to that board meeting, and afterward there was a nice reception for Dan and the three other new elementary school principals in the district. Dan noted that all the other principals in the district attended that board meeting, so he penciled in the first and third Tuesday of every month as an evening when he would be away from home, sitting in on school board meetings.

In July, Dan went to both school board meetings. He wasn't terribly surprised when he saw that he was the only principal in attendance. After all, his more experienced colleagues were probably taking some vacation time. Veterans deserved to miss the ceremonies every once in a while, and as a rookie, he had the right to be "gung ho" the first few months on the job.

When August came around and all the principals in the district were due back for the next school year, Dan again went to both school board meetings. Again, he noted that he was the only building principal in attendance. He expected some recognition from the superintendent, and he hoped that he would earn some "brownie points" for showing up at board meetings. However, there was not even a hint that the superintendent saw him in the middle of the boardroom. Dan had now spent about 14 hours over the past two months attending school board meetings, none of which had even the slightest relevance to his role as a school principal in the district.

Enough was enough. In September, Dan did not attend the first Tuesday board meeting. He decided that staying at home with his family was worth more than the recognition he was likely to get from the central office administrators for being a good company man by attending yet another board meeting. However, when the district principals had their monthly meeting with the assistant superintendent for administrative services on the Wednesday following the first board meeting of the month, Dan was the focus of considerable discussion by some of his colleagues. "Hey, rookie. You didn't make it to the board meeting last night," noted Adam Simitis, one of the more experienced principals in the district. "The superintendent scanned the room and noticed the principals who weren't there. You won't hear anything directly, but the superintendent has a large memory."

Dan felt bad, but he knew that this was the first board meeting of the new school year, so he assumed that he would now be expected to attend board meetings every two weeks. In the third week of September, however, he again appeared at the school board meeting but discovered that he was the only building administrator present. The superintendent again stared blankly at him.

"What the heck am I supposed to do today with the board meetings?" Dan asked Mary Martinez, an elementary school principal who had worked in the district for 10 years. "I show up and I'm the only principal there, so the boss seems to get mad. I don't show up, and I hear the boss also gets mad. Am I being set up for a big fall here, or what?"

Mary smiled at Dan's frustration. "I guess it is hard to walk into a place that's had a history. You've got to be able to read the signs, Dan. When the superintendent wants us to show up at board meetings, such as when the board is scheduled to do anything with the curriculum, select new programs, or review test results, you'd better be there. Otherwise, the boss wants to be the show himself. Read your advance board agenda very carefully on the Friday before the next board meeting."

The revelation about the signs hit Dan like a ton of bricks. From that point on, he figured out the system and didn't miss an important meeting.

CASE STUDY: I'M NOT A POLITICIAN

Karen Chen had been waiting for the past two years to take on her first principalship. Despite many obstacles, she persisted in her efforts to complete a program of studies leading to certification through a local university. She interviewed with several local school districts before she was given her first big chance to become the leader of a small but well-regarded elementary school in a community near home. Like many other school administrators, she found out that she was going to be a new principal just a few weeks before the next school year was to start. Still, she was on cloud nine as August wore on and she got ready for the arrival of her teachers, classified staff, and most important, her students.

Karen was especially looking forward to working with her teachers on a daily basis. For years, as a classroom teacher, she was concerned that principals seemed to be getting further away from their instructional duties. Karen saw her first job as an opening for her to get into a school and truly become an instructional leader. She intended to devote her time to working with students, teachers, staff, and parents in her school. Not only was this a personal goal, but it seemed that it was an idea that was strongly supported by her school district and superintendent. When she stated that her goal was to "take first things first" and improve student learning in her school by working with the people in her school, the interviewing team and superintendent all said that she had exactly the attitude that they wanted to see in a new principal.

Things appeared to be going very well for Karen in her first few weeks as a principal. However, about a month into the school year she received a call from Reverend Dan Adams who explained that he was the president of a local community group that had been formed to ensure that schools would be sensitive to and safeguard traditional family values. It was a pleasant conversation, and Karen explained to Reverend Adams that she appreciated his call, but for the moment she could not become actively involved with organizations that did not work directly with her students, parents, and teachers. After all, she was the principal of a small elementary school in which very few parents were directly involved in Reverend Adams's group. Karen thought to herself that the group headed by Reverend Adams had very little connection with her world and that her time was better spent keeping to her original goals.

As the year progressed, however, Karen received a number of subtle signs from the central office and a few parents in her school to suggest that Reverend Adams's group was not pleased at being turned away from her school. Karen began to understand that what seemed to be a task unconnected to her world as a building instructional leader was having more and more of a negative effect on her daily life as a school administrator.

These three brief scenarios have been selected to illustrate three classic situations representing the kinds of issues faced by many rookie principals. In the first case, Maricela Chavez is a beginning principal faced with the enormous demands of her new job: Papers fill her desk, her superintendent wants answers to every question "right now," and the district policy manual seems to be staring at Maricela in a way that suggests that she had better know every one of its intricate details before she dares to do anything or else she would be perceived as an incompetent rookie. It makes little difference that she has prior experience as an assistant principal. Things are very different in a place where she is "on her own."

Research related to the needs and concerns of beginning principals has shown that Maricela's concerns are common. They are often referred to as the "technical" or "managerial" side of the principalship. They involve the operational details that provide clear direction and order for a school. Some might even say that these skills are needed to "keep the trains running on time." Included may be such tasks as making certain that the policies of the district are followed, that state rules and regulations are addressed, and that the terms of the district's negotiated agreement with teachers are observed.

The technical side of the principalship also involves properly overseeing and maintaining accounts and the school budget, maintaining effective relations with parents and others in the community, developing a weekly schedule of important events and activities, delegating responsibilities to others, keeping student discipline and a safe and orderly physical environment in a school, resolving disputes, and ensuring that all terms of the district's master contract or negotiated agreement with the teachers' association are always addressed. These technical and managerial issues are often referred to as the "Three B's" ("Beans, Busses, and Budgets") of school administration.

It would be incorrect to leave the discussion of important technical demands of the job without noting that for many beginning principals, a major stumbling block is not solely the inability to do certain managerial tasks associated with their jobs. In fact, they may be quite skilled at doing some of the things required in their job descriptions. Rather, many beginners have significant problems because they lack strong communication skills: They know what to do, but they cannot communicate to others *why* they must do what they do. That lack of communication involves both written and oral expression skills. The critical issue here is that even the best administrative "technician" with the best ideas and motives for managing the school can fail if others do not understand what is taking place.

What are some of the technical and managerial aspects of your job as a school principal that concern you during the early stage of your career? (For example, have you discovered that you are not terribly confident with budgeting or the use of technology as part of your daily job requirements?)

_____

_____

_____

_____

The second case study, in which Dan Carter had a hard time understanding when he should or should not attend school board meetings, is also representative of problems often reported by novice school principals. In short, the research refers to them as "problems with socialization." These types of concerns are often related to two different points: socialization to the norms and culture within a particular school district (as Dan's case describes), and socialization to the profession of educational administration in general.

Dan Carter was experiencing frustration in his new job because he could not figure out how to read the subtle signs in his new environment. It made sense to him to attend school board meetings, but he could not understand why he was discouraged from being present at some meetings, whereas at other meetings he seemed to be in trouble when he was absent. He could see no rational pattern. What Dan did not appreciate was some of the history that was known to the senior principals in his district.

Not knowing about the culture, traditions, and history of schools and school districts often hinders new principals in their ability to do their jobs. This gets played out in a variety of ways. Informal "dress codes," participation in administration social events (e.g., golf outings, holiday parties), or even how to address the superintendent's secretary (e.g., never use a first name, as opposed to always use a first name) are examples of the little things that a newcomer needs to understand.

List other examples of some of the local traditions, activities, or past practices that you have discovered as part of the culture of your new setting. (For example, perhaps you have already discovered that Fridays in your school are traditionally "dress down" days for staff, or that teachers do not talk business at the table during lunch.)

_____

_____

_____

_____

The second type of socialization problem often faced by new principals is found in learning about the culture of the principalship as a career. We are talking about trying to understand the big picture of how principals are supposed to act, what they are supposed to know, and even what they are supposed to do, when compared with their colleagues across the United States. Perhaps the best way to summarize this area is with the question, "So what does a principal look like?"

Many new principals become so focused on surviving their first years on the job that they ignore the importance of learning what is going on in the professional world outside their own vision. They are often unaware of the critical issues that colleagues in their own state and across the nation are facing. In recent years, it has been amazing to see the number of principals who were blindsided by issues that were faced by principals in other parts of the country. An example might be the ways in which community pressure groups have focused on such seemingly harmless curricular innovations as outcomes-based education and made these practices the center of considerable controversy. It is understandable that local principals feel as if they must tend to local issues first. However, at the same time, national trends are under way that will eventually affect the local scene. The fact that beginning principals are not being socialized to the larger profession often makes continuing communication with the "outside world" a serious problem.

In the space below, jot down a few additional issues that you have discovered are faced by other principals across the United States and that you now must face in your school or district during your first few years on the job. (For example, has your school or district had to address the issue of allowing prayers in school? What about school safety? How are other principals across the United States addressing the challenges associated with the No Child Left Behind mandates? How do people work with large numbers of students now entering the country from traditional Third World countries?)

_____

_____

_____

_____

The third case was that of Karen Chen, the new principal who was surprised to discover that her work as an elementary principal would also need to include some time to link with important groups in the community, despite her personal vision. She could not maintain her personalized image of the principal being involved only with the business taking place within the walls of her school building. Although it may not have been part of her personal vision of the principalship, she was learning that certain political responsibilities are also part of her "turf."

Researchers have found this viewpoint in many beginning principals. Often, it is connected with becoming effectively socialized to a new role or having an awareness of self. Sometimes new principals are faced with critical decisions that might conflict with their own personal values or ethics. For example, a beginning principal may face the responsibility of evaluating a teacher and know that the evaluation process may end in the nonrenewal or termination of that teacher's position. Is it really in accordance with one's values and ability to carry out a process that may deprive a colleague of his or her career as a teacher?

In a related situation, a new principal may observe teachers who are not performing effectively, but upon reviewing personnel files find nothing but "excellent" or even "superior" ratings provided by the previous principal. Are the perceptions of the new principal incorrect? Have these teachers suddenly become ineffective during the last few months? Or was the previous principal too lenient or unable (or unwilling) to evaluate teachers effectively? Couple this issue with the need for a newcomer to avoid alienating experienced teachers too quickly, and another important conflict for a novice administrator quickly appears.

All these issues surround the image of what it means to be a principal. In Chapter 12, we consider some other ways in which a beginning principal must appreciate his or her role as a boss. It is clear, on the basis of many studies of principals, that people often suffer a kind of shock when their personal value system is suddenly threatened by the kinds of things that they are called upon to do. Can you think of any examples of how your personal awareness of what you might do as a principal has been different from what you expected of that role?

_____

_____

_____

_____

BALANCE IS THE KEY

In the preceding pages, I described some of the problem areas identified by many researchers in the professional lives of beginning principals. A review of these broad areas—technical skills, socialization, and self-awareness or role awareness—often leads a person to try to generalize which area is most important if one is to succeed in the principalship. I must emphasize here that research on beginning principals has shown consistently that all three areas are important. In some ways, that makes your job even harder. It is not possible to simply take care of business by doing nothing more than addressing technical skills for the first year or two, for example. This type of logic is often expressed by novices who state that they want to get established as good managers first, with the assumption that they can take care of other matters (e.g., socialization and self-awareness) at some time in the future.

Research related to the critical skills that should be demonstrated by successful beginning principals has looked at how to address the three areas of concern identified earlier. Different groups of educational administrators were asked to indicate their perceptions of the relative importance of certain job tasks that were, in turn, classified as belonging to technical skills, socialization skills, or self-awareness skills. When principals with at least five years of experience were asked to rate the importance of individual tasks for success and survival by beginning colleagues, they rank the three critical skills in the following way:

1. Socialization skills (most important)

2. Self-awareness and role awareness skills

3. Technical and managerial skills (least important)

When superintendents who had recently hired at least one new principal for their districts were asked the same question, they ranked the skills as follows:

1. Self-awareness and role awareness skills

2. Socialization skills

3. Technical and managerial skills

Finally, those who were enrolled in university programs leading to certification or licensure ranked the three areas as follows:

1. Technical skills

2. Socialization skills

3. Self-awareness and role awareness skills

These findings suggest something very important to recognize about the nature of issues faced by beginning principals. First, some important differences in the rankings show up clearly. Those who have little or no experience as school principals rate technical skills as the most critical issue that needs to be addressed to be successful. However, as people become experienced as administrators, they may downgrade the importance of technical skills and identify socialization and self-awareness (coupled with appreciating the expectations of others) as being more critical to effectiveness, or they develop skills in delegating some technical skills to others. They realize that although the technical side of the job is important, it does not necessarily mean that it must consume the complete attention of the principal all the time.

Second, whatever the differences may be when comparing one group's perceptions with another, no group indicated that any of the three skill areas is unimportant. In other words, experienced administrators may not indicate that managerial and technical skills are as important as the other areas, but they still include as important the performance of the technical aspects of the principalship. Socialization and self-awareness are more important, but no one should assume that daily managerial duties should not be carried out.

The key to effectiveness and survival is to develop a proper balance among the three critical skill areas. The principal must manage the school (i.e., technical and managerial skills), pay attention to fitting in (i.e., socialization), and demonstrate he or she knows what the job is all about and how it affects the individual (self-awareness and role awareness).

SUGGESTIONS FOR IMPROVEMENT AND PROFESSIONAL DEVELOPMENT

Activities that you might carry out to assist you in your professional development in the three critical skill areas include the following:

Technical and Managerial Skills

- Seek an experienced principal in your district to be a job coach who can share some tricks of the trade for more effectively doing some of the technical and managerial parts of your job.
- Consider participating in a leadership assessment activity sponsored by the National Association of Secondary School Principals (NASSP), the National Association of Elementary School Principals (NAESP), your state administrators' association, or your state department of education. This kind of activity will provide insights into your personal strengths and areas needing further development in leadership and management skills. (You may also wish to complete the "Skill Development Inventory" in the Appendix.)
- Make an agreement with one or more experienced principals in your area to visit their schools and shadow them as they engage in the daily management tasks associated with their jobs.
- Consult with principals who served your school before you arrived to learn about critical issues. Pick the brains of other key actors (i.e., teachers, students, classified staff, parents, other community members) to learn about their expectations of the principal.
- If you are lucky enough to find an experienced secretary outside your door, or if you find teachers with whom you can develop rapport, ask them for their insights into the kinds of technical and managerial issues that merit special attention in your school.
- Volunteer to take a "guided tour" of your school with some of the people who know a lot about the "behind the scenes" reality of your building. These people might include custodial staff, security officers, and cafeteria staff. These tours can enable you to appreciate some of the many issues and problems that may call for technical expertise.
- Review some of the practical tips presented in Chapter 4.
- Identify short workshops or seminars related to more effective performance of the technical aspects of the job that are sponsored by local, state, or national organizations.

Socialization

- Work with your job coach and ask questions about the traditions, past practices, and culture of your school and school district.

- Read carefully a random selection of past local school board agendas and minutes to determine whether patterns of practice emerge that you need to learn about.
- Go out of your way to attend lunches, breakfasts, and other social events that might enable you to gain greater insights into some of the shared concerns of your colleagues.
- Spend time getting to know the personality and characteristics of the community within your school. Get to know students, staff, and teachers as people, not simply as people who come into "your" school each day. After all, the faster it becomes "our" school, the better.
- Listen and watch in the ways described in Chapter 7.
- Become an active participant in activities and events sponsored by professional associations of school administrators. Read such publications as the NASSP *Bulletin* and *Principal* published by NAESP.
- Work to learn about the "internal and external" realities of your school. Pay attention to and learn about existing (and possible) connections to social service agencies and how to respond to your police department's demands regarding safety issues. Think about how you will respond to zero tolerance policies that are meant to dictate how you will deal with critical discipline issues.

Self-Awareness and Role Awareness Skills

- Identify a personal mentor within either your school district or some other school system to give you feedback about your career development. This person may or may not be the same person selected as a job coach to help you learn more about technical skills.
- Write and then periodically review your statement of personal professional values or educational philosophy. Further information about this activity is presented in Chapter 12.
- Work with a trusted colleague who will agree to observe your work over a period of time and ask you to describe what you believe you were doing on the job. Compare and contrast your perceptions with those of someone looking at you from the outside.
- Consider how you will address the personal stress you will face as you try to balance your time, your job responsibilities, and your commitment to your family and personal life.

BUILDING A PERSONAL PLAN

In the spaces provided on the next few pages, begin the process of developing a personal professional growth plan, or portfolio, by reflecting on the key concepts addressed in this chapter and specifying some important goals that you might have related to each major issue. For each goal or set of goals, you need to identify activities that will assist you in achieving these goals. Always note the ways in which you can assess your progress toward these goals and objectives.

Area 1: Technical and Managerial Skill Development

Personal objectives for the next year:

_____

_____

_____

_____

Some of the things you will do to achieve these objectives:

_____

_____

_____

_____

The ways in which someone will be able to tell whether you have achieved your objectives:

_____

_____

_____

_____

Area 2: Socialization Skill Development

Personal objectives for the next year:

_____

_____

_____

_____

Some of the things you will do to achieve these objectives:

_____

_____

_____

_____

The ways in which someone will be able to tell whether you have achieved your objectives:

_____

_____

_____

_____

Area 3: Self-Awareness and Role Awareness Skill Development

Personal objectives for the next year:

_____

_____

_____

_____

Some of the things you will do to achieve these objectives:

_____

_____

_____

_____

The ways in which someone will be able to tell whether you have achieved your objectives:

_____

_____

_____

_____

REFERENCE

Wolcott, H. (1973). *The man in the principal's office: An ethnography.* New York: Holt, Rinehart & Winston.

PART I

Technical and Managerial Skills

The next six chapters are devoted to the improvement of your technical and managerial skills. As noted in Chapter 2, if you are beginning the principal-ship, developing these skills is probably your highest priority. Although research supports the fact that you will also need to learn about socialization and self-awareness, the material included in this section should be helpful to you in addressing what may come first in your life at this time.

3

A Personal Leadership Checklist

Roosevelt Autry was enjoying his first year as the principal of Avon Hills High School. For the past four years he had been one of the assistant principals at the school, and he had the opportunity to learn about the teachers, students, parents, and members of the community. It was not a surprise when he was named the principal; he knew the school, and the community knew him.

As Roosevelt moved through his first year, he remained quite comfortable with his assignment, for the most part. In many ways, it was a continuation of what he had done in the past although he knew that being the principal would carry a lot more pressure and responsibility than his former job. But things seemed to be running smoothly. On the other hand, Roosevelt often went home at the end of the day feeling as if something was missing from this year's experience. He was far from being overconfident about how he was doing as the leader of his school. He was sure that others watching his performance would say that he had a good start at becoming a good principal. Avon Hills was "working" pretty well, but Roosevelt wished he could get some sense of how well he was really doing.

Roosevelt Autry is not unusual. Too often, beginning principals invest so much time in finding their first job, getting the school year started, and keeping their buildings open and well-maintained that they often have little or no opportunity to check out the effectiveness of their work. Are they doing a good job? Or are they simply staying one step ahead of the next serious crisis that will land on their desks? School districts, of course, have timelines and procedures to be followed in the evaluation of their administrative personnel. However, these evaluative procedures are often cast in a way that is tied to either merit pay decisions or content decisions. Often, a beginning principal can hear that he or she is doing an acceptable or even "above average" job, but that same principal still is puzzled as to whether he or she is doing the job intended.

Typical evaluation practices for school administrators are designed to assess whether people are doing their jobs, not whether they are growing professionally and becoming more effective leaders. The result is that principals, whether at the beginning of their careers or after they have had a lot of experience, rarely get any insights into the effectiveness of their work during a school year. I believe this is unfortunate because it promotes the notion that principals, particularly those who are new to the job, are meant to direct their efforts toward survivorship and not leadership.

This chapter provides you with an opportunity to reflect on your own leadership style and skills and compare them with the effective educational leadership that is presented in current research literature. The most important process is the expectation that you will conclude your review of the material presented here by identifying some of your personal strengths and limitations. In turn, these may serve as yet another part of your personal professional portfolio. The goal here is not to indicate where you have problems. Rather, you should be clear about the ways in which you can enhance your role as an educational leader.

CRITICAL LEADERSHIP SKILLS

The number of lists that contain statements of specific skills reportedly needed by effective leaders is probably as large as the number of people who have become leaders over the years. Some of the lists included here that are relevant to the discussion are those prepared by the Association for Supervision and Curriculum Development (ASCD, 1989), Stephen R. Covey (1991), Warren Bennis and Burt Nanus (1985), the National Association of Elementary School Principals (NAESP, 1991), the National Association of Secondary School Principals (NASSP, 2004), and the Interstate School Leaders Licensure Consortium (1996).

The ASCD (1989) notes that effective educational leaders do the following:

1. **They provide a sense of vision to their schools**. They demonstrate the ability to articulate what a school is supposed to do, particularly in terms of what it should do to benefit children.

2. **They engage in participative management**. They encourage a better organizational climate in the school by allowing teachers and staff to participate meaningfully in real decision making and not merely in an effort to "play at" getting people involved when decisions have already been made.

3. **They provide support for instruction.** Instructional leaders are so committed to maintaining quality instruction as their primary organizational focus that when decisions must be made concerning priorities, instruction always comes first.

4. **They monitor instruction.** They know what is going on in the classrooms of their schools.

5. **They are resourceful.** Instructional leaders rarely allow circumstances in their organization to get in the way of their vision for quality educational programs.

Stephen Covey (1991) noted the following characteristics of what he refers to as "principle-centered leaders":

1. **They are continually learning.** Principle-centered leaders are constantly educated by their experiences.

2. **They are service oriented.** Those striving to be principle-centered leaders see life as a mission.

3. **They radiate positive energy.** Principle-centered people are cheerful, pleasant, and happy.

4. **They believe in other people.** Principle-centered people don't overreact to negative behaviors, criticisms, or human weaknesses.

5. **They lead balanced lives.** They read the best literature and magazines and keep up with current affairs and events.

6. **They see life as an adventure.** Principle-centered people savor life; they have no need to categorize or stereotype people and events.

7. **They are synergistic.** Principle-centered people serve as change catalysts in organizations, and they improve most situations in which they become involved.

8. **They exercise for self-renewal.** They regularly exercise the four dimensions of the human personality: physical, mental, emotional, and spiritual.

Warren Bennis and Burt Nanus (1985) noted that successful leaders engage in the following five strategies:

Strategy 1: Attention Through Vision. Leaders develop a focus in an organization or in an agenda that demonstrates an unparalleled concern for outcomes, products, and results.

Strategy 2: Meaning Through Communication. Effective communication is inseparable from effective leadership.

Strategy 3: Trust Through Positioning. Leaders must be trusted in order to be effective; we trust people who are predictable and whose positions are known. Leaders who are trusted make themselves known and make their positions clear.

Strategy 4: Deployment of Self Through Positive Self-Renewal. Leaders have positive self-images and self-regard that are not self-centered, and they know their worth. In general, they are confident without being cocky.

Strategy 5: Deployment of Self Through the "Wallenda Factor." Before his death, the famous aerialist Karl Wallenda was said to have become more preoccupied with not failing than succeeding. Leaders are able to consistently focus their energies on success.

Now that you have reviewed the lists of critical skills for leaders that have been identified by ASCD, Covey, and Bennis and Nanus, select two or three of these skills that you believe others could identify in your style of work as a school principal:

_____

_____

_____

_____

Now, review the three lists again and select two or three skills that you believe may be seen as shortcomings in your style:

_____

_____

_____

_____

Another list of critical leadership skills has been developed by NAESP (2002). These skills are different from the others we have reviewed. They are designed to enable school principals to review the skills they believe may need further refinement and improvement. As you consider each leadership area, take time to assess your own performance in this area as a central competency of your work.

Area 1: Leadership Behavior

The principal must

1. Exercise vision and promote leadership that appropriately involves staff, students, and the community and the identification and accomplishment of the school's mission.

Your personal level of proficiency in this skill:

_____

_____

2. Recognize the individual needs of all staff and students, including those who are at risk because of diverse cultures, backgrounds, and abilities.

Your personal level of proficiency in this skill:

_____

_____

3. Apply effective human relations skills.

Your personal level of proficiency in this skill:

_____

_____

4. Encourage and develop the leadership of others.

Your personal level of proficiency in this skill:

_____

_____

5. Analyze relevant information, make decisions, delegate responsibility, and provide appropriate support and follow-up.

Your personal level of proficiency in this skill:

_____

_____

6. Identify and creatively coordinate the use of available human, material, and financial resources to achieve the school's missions and goals.

Your personal level of proficiency in this skill:

_____

_____

7. Explore, assess, develop, and implement educational concepts that enhance teaching and learning.

Your personal level of proficiency in this skill:

_____

_____

8. Band the community together through shared vision and beliefs.

Your personal level of proficiency in this skill:

_____

_____

9. Initiate and manage constructive change.

Your personal level of proficiency in this skill:

_____

_____

10. Participate actively as a member of local, state, and national professional groups.

Your personal level of proficiency in this skill:

_____

_____

Area 2: Communication Skills

The principal must

1. Articulate beliefs persuasively, effectively defend decisions, explain innovations, and behave in ways that are congruent with these beliefs and decisions.

Your personal level of proficiency in this skill:

_____

_____

2. Write clearly and concisely so that the message is understood by the intended audiences.

Your personal level of proficiency in this skill:

_____

_____

3. Utilize basic facts and data and recognize values when communicating priorities.

Your personal level of proficiency in this skill:

_____

_____

4. Demonstrate skills in nonverbal communication, including personal impact, to communicate a positive image of the school.

Your personal level of proficiency in this skill:

_____

_____

5. Use current technologies to communicate the school's philosophy, mission, needs, and accomplishments.

Your personal level of proficiency in this skill:

_____

_____

6. Make effective use of mass media.

Your personal level of proficiency in this skill:

_____

_____

7. Use active listening skills.

Your personal level of proficiency in this skill:

_____

_____

8. Express disagreement without being disagreeable.

Your personal level of proficiency in this skill:

_____

_____

9. Promote student and staff use of higher-level thinking skills.

Your personal level of proficiency in this skill:

_____

_____

10. Exemplify the behavior expected in others.

Your personal level of proficiency in this area:

_____

_____

11. Keep communication flowing to and from the school.

Your personal level of proficiency in this skill:

_____

_____

12. Communicate with the various constituencies within the school community.

Your personal level of proficiency in this skill:

_____

_____

Area 3: Group Processes

The principal must

1. Apply the principles of group dynamics and facilitation skills.

Your personal level of proficiency in this skill:

_____

_____

2. Involve staff, parents, students, and the community in setting goals.

Your personal level of proficiency in this skill:

_____

_____

3. Resolve difficult situations by the use of conflict resolution skills.

Your personal level of proficiency in this skill:

_____

_____

4. Match the appropriate decision-making techniques to the particular situation.

Your personal level of proficiency in this skill:

_____

_____

5. Identify—in collaboration with staff, students, and parents—the decision-making procedures the school will follow.

Your personal level of proficiency in this skill:

_____

_____

6. Apply the process of consensus-building both as a leader and as a member of a group.

Your personal level of proficiency in this skill:

_____

_____

7. Achieve intended outcomes through the use of principles of motivation.

Your personal level of proficiency in this skill:

_____

_____

In addition to these proficiencies related to the leadership responsibilities of school principals, NAESP suggests you may wish to review your performance in the following areas as well.

Supervisory Proficiencies

1. Curriculum
2. Instruction
3. Performance
4. Evaluation

Administrative and Management Competencies

1. Organizational Management
2. Fiscal Management
3. Political Management

NAESP (2002) has recently developed another set of "Standards for What Principals Should Know and Be Able to Do." Read over the following descriptions of the standards along with strategies that effective principals have recommended as ways to achieve these goals. After each standard, you may wish to jot down some of the ways in which you have already met each item, or intend to work toward it during this next year.

Standard One: Lead Schools in a Way That Places Students and Adult Learning at the Center

Strategies:

- Create and foster a community of learners
- Embody learner-centered leadership
- Seek leadership contributions from multiple sources
- Tie the daily operation of the schoolhouse to school and student learning goals

Your personal reaction to Standard One:

_____

_____

_____

_____

Standard Two: Set High Expectations and Standards for the Academic and Social Development of All Students and the Performance of Adults

Strategies:

- Articulate a clear vision that reflects the beliefs, values, and commitments of the school community
- Ensure that all students have adequate and appropriate opportunities to meet high standards
- Develop a school culture that is flexible, collaborative, innovative, and supportive of efforts to improve achievement of all students

Your personal reaction to Standard Two:

_____

_____

_____

_____

Standard Three: Demand Content and Instruction That Ensure Student Achievement of Agreed-Upon Academic Standards

Strategies:

- Hire and retain high quality teachers and hold them responsible for student learning
- Monitor alignment of curriculum with standards, school goals, and assessment
- Observe classroom practices to ensure that all students are meaningfully engaged in active learning
- Provide up-to-date technology with instructional materials
- Review and analyze student work to determine whether students are being taught to standard

Your personal reaction to Standard Three:

_____

_____

_____

_____

_____

Standard Four: Create a Culture of Continuous Learning for Adults Tied to Student Learning and Other School Goals

Strategies:

- Provide time for reflection as an important part of improving practice
- Invest in teacher learning
- Connect professional development to school learning goals
- Provide opportunities for teachers to work, plan, and think together
- Recognize the need to continually improve principals' own professional development

Your personal reaction to Standard Four:

_____

_____

_____

_____

_____

Standard Five: Use Multiple Sources of Data as Diagnostic Tools to Assess, Identify, and Apply Instructional Improvement

Strategies:

- Consider a variety of sources to measure performance
- Analyze data using a variety of strategies
- Use data as tools to identify barriers to success, design strategies for improvement, and plan daily instruction
- Benchmark successful schools with familiar demographics to identify strategies for improving student achievement
- Create a school environment that is comfortable using data

Your personal reaction to Standard Five:

_____

_____

_____

_____

Standard Six: Actively Engage the Community to Create Shared Responsibility for Student and School Success

Strategies:

- Engage the community to build greater ownership for the work of the school
- Share leadership and decision making
- Encourage parents to become meaningfully involved in the school and in their own children's learning
- Ensure that students and families are connected to the health, human, and social services they need to stay focused on learning

Your personal reaction to Standard Six:

_____

_____

_____

_____

Several years ago, the National Association of Secondary School Principals (NASSP) derived another framework from its Assessment Center skill areas (Schmitt, Joe, Merritt, Fitzgerald, & Jorgenson, 1982). You may wish to periodically review the extent to which you are demonstrating these competencies. This may be an important and useful technique to guide your personal leadership checkup.

Administrative Skill Dimensions

1. **Problem Analysis**: The ability to seek out relevant data and analyze complex information to determine the important elements of a problem situation.

2. **Judgment:** The ability to reach logical conclusions and make high quality decisions on the basis of available information; skill in identifying educational needs and setting priorities; ability to critically evaluate communication.

3. **Organizational Ability:** The ability to schedule and control the work of others; skill in using resources in an optimal fashion; ability to deal with a volume of paperwork and heavy demands on one's time.

4. **Leadership:** The ability to get others involved in solving problems, to recognize when a group requires direction, and to interact effectively with a group and guide them to accomplish a task.

5. **Sensitivity:** The ability to perceive the needs, concerns, and personal problems of others; tact in dealing with persons from different backgrounds; ability to deal with people concerning emotional issues; awareness of what information to communicate and to whom.

6. **Decisiveness:** The ability to recognize when a decision is required and act quickly.

7. **Range of interests:** Competence to discuss a variety of topics—educational, political, current events, economics, and so on; active participation in events.

8. **Personal Motivation:** The need to achieve in all activities; evidence that work is important to personal satisfaction; ability to be self-policing.

9. **Educational Values:** Possession of a well-reasoned educational philosophy; receptiveness to new ideas.

10. **Stress Tolerance:** The ability to perform under pressure and during opposition; the ability to think on one's feet.

11. **Oral Communication:** The ability to make clear oral presentations of facts or ideas.

12. **Written Communication:** The ability to express ideas clearly in writing; to write appropriately for different audiences—students, parents, and so on.

13. **Conflict Management:** The willingness to intervene in conflict situations and the ability to develop solutions that are agreeable to all persons involved.

14. **Political Astuteness:** The ability to perceive critical features of the environment such as power structure, political players, and special interest groups; the ability to formulate alternatives that reflect realistic expectations.

15. **Risk Taking:** The extent to which calculated risks are taken on the basis of sound judgments.

16. **Creativity:** The ability to generate ideas that provide new and different solutions to management problems or opportunities.

As you read through these 16 competencies, on which areas do you believe that you would like to focus some attention for personal improvement?

_____

_____

_____

_____

For each of these areas in which you would like to improve your performance, what are some specific strategies that you may follow as part of a plan for personal improvement? (For example, if one of the skill areas identified for improvement is written communication, you may wish to enroll in a writing course at a local community college or simply ask a friend to critique your written memos, letters, etc.)

_____

_____

_____

_____

Research by NASSP (2004) has also identified several leadership behaviors by principals whose schools can be described as particularly effective in terms of promoting greater student learning and achievement. Specifically, leaders of good schools

- Are aggressive in articulating and modeling personal beliefs about the success of each student.
- Understand that teachers are the key individuals who collectively determine the school's quality and that they need involvement, the opportunity for leadership, encouragement, support, and high expectations for the way they think and behave toward the students they teach.
- Establish formal structures (e.g., committees, advisory teams, school improvement teams) to engage teachers and other stakeholders in the decision-making process.
- Identify potential leaders among faculty members and nurture them to become teacher-leaders, and perhaps for some, future principals.
- Read and build knowledge of school improvement, change processes, collaborative and distributive leadership, and efficient daily management.
- Develop confidence among faculty members, students, and parents that the daily operations of the school will go smoothly; implement effective daily operational routines throughout the school; and maintain communication with staff members so they know and follow routines.
- Implement organizational structures that enhance the academic and social success of all students.
- Understand the importance of literacy and mathematics as foundational skills of all students, and do whatever is necessary to provide learning opportunities that prevent students from leaving school without those skills.
- Collect and analyze data that will move the school toward accomplishing its vision and goals, including data about students; the school's environment; instructional practices throughout the school; the attitudes of parents, students, and teachers; and the integrity of the written and taught curriculum.

How do you assess your personal ability to engage in these behaviors? What strategies or activities will you follow and carry out to strengthen your skills related to these areas?

_____

_____

_____

_____

One final framework of critical leadership skills you may wish to consult is one developed by the Interstate School Leaders Licensure Consortium (ISLLC, 1996). This group, supported by the Council of Chief State School Officers (CCSSO), was formed to promote the adoption of national standards to guide the preservice preparation, licensure, and continuing professional development of American educational leaders. The group prepared six broad outcome standards, with corresponding statements of expected knowledge, dispositions, and performance expectations tied to each standard. The six standards are presented below, along with detailed descriptions of the component elements of the first standard.

Standard 1: A school administrator is an educational leader who promotes the success of all students by facilitating the development, articulation, implementation, and stewardship of a vision of learning that is shared and supported by the school community.

KNOWLEDGE: The administrator has knowledge and understanding of

- Learning goals in a pluralistic society
- The principles of developing and implementing strategic plans
- Systems theory
- Information sources, data collection, and data analysis strategies
- Effective communication
- Effective consensus-building and negotiation skills

DISPOSITIONS: The administrator believes in, values, and is committed to

- The educability of all
- A school vision of high standards of learning
- Continuous school improvement
- The inclusion of all members of the school community
- Ensuring that students have the knowledge, skills, and values needed to become successful adults
- A willingness to continuously examine one's own assumptions, beliefs, and practices
- Doing the work required for high levels of personal and organizational performance

PERFORMANCE: The administrator facilitates processes and engages in activities ensuring that

- The missions and vision are communicated through the use of symbols, ceremonies, stories, and similar activities
- The core beliefs of the school vision are modified for all stakeholders
- The vision is developed with and among stakeholders

- The contributions of school community members to the realization of the vision are recognized and celebrated
- Progress toward the vision and mission is communicated to all stakeholders
- The school community is involved in school improvement efforts
- The vision shapes the educational progress, plans, and activities
- An implementation plan is developed in which objectives and strategies to achieve the vision and goals are clearly articulated
- Assessment data related to student learning are used to develop the school vision and goals
- Relevant demographic data pertaining to the students and their families are used in developing the school vision and goals
- Barriers to achieving the vision are identified, clarified, and addressed
- Needed resources are sought and obtained to support the implementation of the school mission and goals
- Existing resources are used in support of the school vision and goals
- The vision, mission, and implementation plans are regularly monitored and revised

Standard 2: A school administrator is an educational leader who promotes the success of all students by advocating, nurturing, and sustaining a school culture and instructional program conducive to student learning and staff professional growth.

Standard 3: A school administrator is an educational leader who promotes the success of all students by ensuring management of the organization, operations, and resources for a safe, efficient, and effective learning environment.

Standard 4: A school administrator is an educational leader who promotes the success of all students by collaborating with families and community members, responding to diverse community interests and needs, and mobilizing community resources.

Standard 5: A school administrator is an educational leader who promotes the success of all students by acting with integrity, fairness, and in an ethical manner.

Standard 6: A school administrator is an educational leader who promotes the success of all students by understanding, responding to, and influencing the larger political, social, economic, legal, and cultural context.

As was the case with other descriptions of important leadership skills, you may wish to list here some areas where you will focus future professional development activity.

_____

_____

_____

_____

YOUR PERSONAL PLAN

An assessment of your leadership skills can serve as an important foundation for a personal portfolio and growth plan. This chapter included several frameworks that have been developed to assist people in analyzing certain research-based competencies needed to lead schools. You may wish to consider these skills, or you may want to consider other issues that you will need to face as a school principal. For example, how effective are you in seeking and securing additional resources for your school? After all, a reality of present-day education is that it will be increasingly critical for educators to become grant writers, because the traditional sources of financial support are often not sufficient to allow schools to reach their goals. Other similar kinds of skills and abilities may also come to mind.

In the space below, identify some of your strengths and some of your weaknesses with regard to the leadership skills identified throughout this chapter. For each item, identify a timeline that you intend to follow in either strengthening that skill or finding ways to increase your personal skills. Note also some of the activities and strategies that you believe may assist you in your improvement effort. (For example, "I will increase the effectiveness of my public speaking and oral communication skills over the next school year by participating in the local Toastmasters' Club and also by volunteering often to make public addresses.")

_____

_____

_____

_____

REFERENCES

Association for Supervision and Curriculum Development. (1989). *Instructional leadership* [Videotape]. Alexandria, VA: Author.

Bennis, W. G., & Nanus, B. (1985). *Leaders: Strategies for taking charge.* New York: Harper & Row.

Covey, S. R. (1991). *Principle-centered leadership: Strategies for personal and professional effectiveness.* New York: Simon & Schuster.

Interstate School Leaders Licensure Consortium. (1996). *Standards for school leaders.* Washington, DC: Council of Chief State School Officers.

National Association of Elementary School Principals (1991). *Proficiencies for school principals* (Rev. ed.) Alexandria, VA: Author.

National Association of Elementary School Principals. (2002). *Leading learning communities: Standards for what principals should know and be able to do.* Alexandria, VA: Author.

National Association of Elementary School Principals, Educational Research Service, & National Association of Secondary School Principals. (2002). *K–12 principals guide to "No Child Left Behind."* Reston, VA: Author.

National Association of Secondary School Principals. (2004). *Breaking ranks II: Strategies for leading school reform.* Reston, VA: Author.

Pristash, S. H. (2002). *What people think principals do.* Lanham, MD: Scarecrow Press.

Schmitt, N., Joe, R., Merritt, R., Fitzgerald, M., & Jorgenson, C. (1982). *Criterion-related and content validity of the NASSP assessment center.* Reston, VA: National Association of Secondary School Principals.

Snow, A. L. (2004). *More practical advice for principals.* Lanham, MD: Scarecrow Press.

Valentine, J. W., Clark, D. C., Hackmann, D. G., & Petzko, V. N. (2004). *Leadership for highly successful middle level school: A national study of leadership in middle level schools.* Reston, VA: National Association of Secondary School Principals.

4

Expectations for Technical and Managerial Skills

Esteban Perez stood in front of Martin Avenue Elementary School with a key to the building in his right hand and suddenly realized that he would be the principal of this school—at least for the next year of his life. Esteban's route to this point had taken him from six years as a primary school teacher to two years as an at-risk coordinator in the same school. Five years ago, he took his first job as an assistant principal at Sunshine Hollow Middle School. Last spring, Esteban applied for principalships that were advertised in five different school districts close to where he had worked for the past 13 years. In total, he went through an even dozen interviews with different groups of parents, teachers, central office administrators, community group members, students, and school board members. In some cases he had done well; in a few situations he had really bombed out. So when he finally got a phone call asking him to take over here at Martin Avenue, he leaped at the chance to prove that he could do a great job as the principal.

Today, however, he had feelings of apprehension as he walked through the front door of his new school. He learned a lot about administration through his work as an at-risk coordinator and as an assistant principal. He had a particularly good role model as his principal at Sunshine Hollow. Now, however, Esteban realized that he was no longer "flying the plane from the right seat" as an assistant principal. He was now the pilot, the one in charge, and he was responsible for making things happen at his school.

As he settled in at the desk in his new office, Esteban Perez started to sift through the enormous pile of papers that were laid neatly in his in-basket by Martha Delvecchio, his secretary. She now stood before him, notebook and pencil in hand, waiting for directions concerning the order of business to be followed during the next few weeks before the beginning of the new school year. In that way, she and Esteban could develop a tickler file that they could consult each day to remind them of events that needed to be addressed as the year progressed.

Esteban thought Maria's idea was a good one, but he realized that although there were many things he needed to learn about the new school, the new school system, and the new job, he had not given much thought to what technical skills and practices were needed to make this a successful first year as principal.

Esteban's situation is not unique. Often people spend so much time thinking about how to do individual tasks associated with the principalship (e.g., how to manage the building budget, how to observe and evaluate teachers, or how to pay attention to legal mandates) that they never think in terms of the big picture of leading a school for an entire year. Alternatively, they also frequently find themselves in situations much like Esteban's: They spend a lot of time working toward getting their first job and then walk into the position without really knowing how to carry out their responsibilities. This is true even in cases where rookie principals have had successful prior experience as assistant principals. These are realistic situations that beginners often face, and they are concerns not often remembered by experienced colleagues who often do things on the basis of their experience.

SOME APPARENT CONTRADICTIONS

The most critical skill to be addressed by any beginning principal is to develop an appreciation for personal values and beliefs. As a result, this chapter might seem contradictory because it looks at the technical and managerial skills needed for principals to succeed in their jobs. Often, people speak of administrative skills in a negative way. They talk about the "three B's of school administration: beans, busses, and budgets" with a sort of disdain that suggests that schools cannot go without food, transportation, or money. The implication is that being an effective leader is something well beyond mere management. But a person can never serve as a true leader if he or she does not also survive as a manager. The job has to be done.

This chapter looks at the technical and managerial side of the principal's job. The goal here is to present an overview of the many tasks that need to be done each year by school principals and to work with you to set up a schedule for carrying out these tasks. Some of the items might be classified as formal or mandated activities that are required by state law, collective bargaining agreements, or local school board policy. Exact dates will vary in different school districts or states. Other important technical duties need to be performed by effective principals even if they are not officially required.

FORMAL REQUIREMENTS

You must do a number of things each year because they are formal requirements of the job. If you miss the deadlines associated with these tasks, you might be in violation of contracts, local policies, or even state and local laws. As a result, these items cannot be allowed to simply slip once in a while. You could lose your job or be held personally and legally liable if you do not meet these deadlines and due dates.

Deadlines are important, but they are generally listed in formal memos, the district's weekly calendar of events, job descriptions, board policies, and a wide array of other places that will make them relatively hard to forget or ignore. Few principals are wholly unprepared for the fact that, for example, they must complete the evaluation of all untenured teachers in their schools by a certain date. This is an example of an important technical and managerial task that you must address, but it is far from the subtle issue that is easy to forget most of the time.

INFORMAL TASKS

Informal tasks are the things you will not necessarily find listed in the local school district's board policy manual or in the education code for your state or even in the terms of the negotiated contract for your local teachers' association. However, failure to do some of these things might make a difference to how you are able to carry out your job as a principal. They are the kinds of things that—as experienced principals have discovered over the years—make the school year run a lot more smoothly and reduce tensions and frustrations not only for you but also for your staff, students, and the community with whom you will be working.

The next few pages will list some of the important things—both formal and informal—that need to be done throughout the school year. The lists indicate activities that should be performed before the year begins, during the school year, and toward the end of the year to ensure that next year will be easier than this one. Some suggestions fit nicely and cleanly into one of these three periods; others do not because they must be addressed throughout the year.

BEFORE THE YEAR BEGINS

Most people get their first administrative assignments during the summer, before the new school year begins. In an ideal world, you might be selected as a principal in May or June, with an understanding that your contract officially begins on July 1 and that teachers will be back by early or mid-August, two or three weeks before students arrive. In that ideal world, then, you might have a few months to plan for the upcoming school year; check over your school; learn about the students, teachers, staff, and school district; and so on. In the real world, however, you might receive your first principalship only a few weeks (or days) before the school year begins.

Regardless of the situation in which you find yourself, you can do a number of things in the months, weeks, or even days before teachers and students walk into your school. These activities are classified in several different areas: building preparation; instructional management; materials and supplies; communications with staff, students, parents, and community; and finally, perhaps most critical, personal preparation.

Building Preparation Activities

The following activities may help you to prepare for your first year in the principalship:

- Walk around your school with your chief custodian and check out the overall cleanliness and state of repair; notify the custodial staff of areas needing attention. While making your assessment, develop a priority system to indicate what things must be done first. For example, are there immediate health and safety concerns? What about things that affect instruction? Comfort for students, teachers, and staff? Appearance? (Remember that most people in your community get to know what is going on in your school. Their judgment of the quality of a school is based largely on "drive by" assessments of cleanliness, order, and so forth.)
- Examine the lighting around the school (interior and exterior). Walk around your school's exterior in the evening to check for "dark spots" that could be unsafe for visitors or students staying around for sporting events.
- Look over such often-forgotten but important areas as ventilation, signs of water damage, plumbing problems, and electrical hazards.
- Learn about your building's fire alarm system and security systems and how to arm them, override them, and even disconnect them if necessary.
- Verify that things ordered by the previous principal were actually done in your building for this year (e.g., were structural changes, repairs, etc., actually carried out by your custodial staff or outside contractors?).
- Check the external conditions of your building during the summer months—and remember that the outside of your building, including the grounds around it, is what the public sees every day.
- Update teacher and staff mail locations to reflect new staff members. (Remember that you probably won't be the only "new kid" in school next year. Making certain that little things like mailbox arrangements are taken care of is a way to avoid annoying the teachers who are familiar with the way things "are supposed to be.")
- Learn about your building's idiosyncrasies, hidden rooms, and so forth. (This is particularly an adventure in older buildings, or areas where several wings have been added over the years. Often, you will find small closets in gyms, auditoriums, and other similar areas of the school.)
- Contact your district's security or local police department and have them lead you through a safety audit of your campus. (This is, unfortunately, a precaution needed in the time we now face in many public institutions, including schools. The aim here is to inform you, not frighten anybody!)
- Form a relationship with your district's supervisor or administrator. (This person can get you through some tough confrontations with reluctant custodians or repair people.)
- Contact the appropriate central office personnel to determine whether any major repair or remodeling projects are scheduled for your campus this year. (I recall the unfortunate example of a beginning high school principal who arrived at her school on the first day of classes to discover workers spreading hot tar on the roof of her building. The roofing project had been scheduled for completion three weeks earlier, but weather conditions "forced" the work to be done when it was now taking place. A sympathetic district administrator

quickly moved the work crew to another project until the first week of a new school year was over.)

- Do whatever you and your staff can do to make the building as neat, clean, safe, and attractive as possible for the first day that your teachers return. (This little action will have a big boost for teacher morale.)
- Arrange your office so that it reflects you and your personal style: move the desk, put up photos and plants, and so forth. (This strategy really tells people a lot about you very quickly.)
- Check out your school's recorded messages on the telephone to ensure that all information is accurate and that you can provide the same information to callers and visitors.
- Visit your school's Web site and review all information for accuracy.
- Walk out in front of your school and take a look at the building and grounds. Would you be proud to send your own child to the place you see? If not, what changes need to be made?

Instructional Management

- If you are new to your district, or if you have come from another state, review your local policies and practices related to conforming to the mandates in IDEA legislation and No Child Left Behind (NCLB).
- Review your school's performance and the previous three years of standardized testing and other measures of effectiveness of schools in your district and state. (For example, you may wish to review past discipline data, dropout rates, and truancy data.)
- As you review performance data from recent school years, note any discernible trends related to student group populations in your school. (Is there any evidence that one or more subgrouping of students are performing at unacceptably low levels?)
- Review inservice activities that were carried out in the past to assist your teachers in addressing any instructional concerns in your school. Make certain to work carefully at any evaluative data regarding the perceived effectiveness of the inservice.
- Review your building budget for resources that can be used for additional support for paying teachers for tutoring and for teacher inservice that may be needed.
- If the previous leadership team of your school prepared a school improvement plan that identified instructional goals for this next year, review it to determine what the past vision was. It is up to you to adhere to this plan or not. In any case, it should be a starting point for your own goals.
- Develop a draft statement of what you believe may be appropriate instructional goals for this next school year. Be prepared to share this tentative statement with your teaching staff at the first meeting of the school year.
- If one is not already scheduled, convene a meeting of department chairs, subject leaders, grade level team leaders, or others in similar instructional leadership roles in the school to review last year's test data and begin to develop a school improvement plan for the coming year. (If such a plan already exists, this first meeting of your instructional improvement team or committee would be an ideal time to consider the ways in which the plan will

be implemented this next year. Also, remember that this first meeting is meant only as a starting place. As the year goes on, you may wish to expand membership to include selected parents, staff members, community representatives, and perhaps students.)

Materials and Supplies

- Learn the location of supply closets, storage rooms, and so on.
- Check to see whether materials and equipment ordered last spring were delivered this summer; if not, contact the vendors to find out why.
- Review supplies and materials inventory procedures. (Do this at two levels. First, check out district policies and procedures. Next, be aware of "the way things have always been done" in your school.)
- Make certain that you have an ample supply of forms (e.g., budgeting forms, leave request forms, insurance forms, student discipline referral forms) on hand to start the school year so that you will not have to bother the central office for this type of material just as the new year starts.
- Make certain that such things as student and staff handbooks are ready to be distributed as soon as the new year begins.

Communications With Staff, Parents, Community, and Students

- Send out letters of introduction to parents, teachers, and staff; invite people to stop by your office to meet you during the summer. (This is particularly important for teachers who might not know much about you, where you came from, or a lot of other information that was not generally known by all the teachers and staff during your hiring process.)
- Take your building staff (secretaries, clerks, custodians, cafeteria workers, etc.) out to lunch, or at least make certain to spend a significant amount of one-to-one time with each of these very important people before the school year begins.
- Listen and learn as much as possible about the local culture of your school, your neighborhood, and the school district. Who are some of the local heroes? And are there any legends to learn? (Even if you came to this school from another building in the district, this is an important tip.)
- Meet with the PTA/PTO officers, booster club officers, or any other organized parent groups that will be part of your school community.
- Work with experienced personnel to identify local community groups, individuals, or organizations. (Do not offend important locals.)
- Identify important people in community social service agencies, the police department, and so on. Find time to make personal visits to the people you may need to call on in emergencies after the year starts. (People will remember and always respond more quickly to requests from people they know.)
- Form school-business partnerships, if possible. Maintain any partnerships started in the past.
- Prepare a "Welcome Back" letter to your parents and students and send it out so that it will arrive about a week before the school year officially begins.

(Remember to carefully proofread this letter and all other messages sent from your office so they contain no errors in spelling, punctuation, or grammar. Do not rely on "Spell-Check." Remember that you are on stage every time you send something out into the community.)

- Prepare a "Welcome Back" letter and address it personally to each staff member. Talk about what you want to do in school, but please avoid "educationese."

- Do not pass up invitations to attend important local and traditional events (the superintendent's cookout, the teachers' family picnic, etc.) or seemingly important community festivals (the annual pumpkin parade, "Pickle Fest," rodeo days, etc.). Every one of these events is an opportunity to learn more about the culture and show your sincere interest in the people who will be central to your success.

- Prepare the daily announcements and newsletters for the first week of the school year well in advance of the big day. Also, prepare the agenda for your first teachers' and staff meetings.

- Read local newspapers. Subscribe to one if you live in another community.

- Arrange appointments with all staff and parent leaders prior to the start of the school year. These meetings will be informal "get to know you" sessions that might include three important questions: (1) What makes you most proud of our school? (2) What do you value most about our school? and (3) What would you like to see changed at our school so that it can be even better? Answers to these questions may give you a quick overview of what can or should be changed as soon as possible, what "sacred cows" exist for you to live with for awhile, and what strengths you can build on during the next year or two.

- After reviewing the personnel files of all your teachers and staff members, note any situations where people may have been put on some type of "growth plan" or other similar disciplinary action by your predecessor. Arrange individual sessions with each of these people to alert them to the fact that you are aware of their situation. Let them talk about their cases, and listen attentively. Make no threats, promises, or guarantee other than to respect the terms of the growth plan and be fair.

Curriculum

- Learn the teaching culture of the school. Are teams used? Are there teachers who have always excelled as loners? Who will work well with whom?

- Review the district curriculum, graded course of study (if one exists), and scope and sequence; make certain that teachers have copies of, or at least access to, curriculum guides (as mandated by local or state policy).

- Learn about special education or inclusion programs that are followed in the department, and consider the implications for your building. If possible, meet the director of special education for your district and share your previous experience with this important individual. (Do this even if you have never had any contact with special education in the past. You will need to learn quickly, so having an ally in "high places" can help down the road.)

- Meet with the district's director of curriculum to learn about additional specifics of curriculum planning and development in your system.

Personal Preparation

- Read those journals that you previously put aside and learn about some major trends in education that you might be facing as a principal. (Many things that seemed irrelevant to you when were a teacher, counselor, special project director, or assistant principal may now have major consequences for your leadership role as a principal.)
- Consider investing in a subscription to *Education Week.*
- Talk to people to learn about special school traditions, events, and customs.
- Set up a tentative monthly plan of events for this next year. Set up a tickler file to remind you of significant deadlines or timelines that you will need to meet or follow.
- Set up your personal phone filing system on your desk; program speed dials for frequent phone numbers; record a personal greeting for your voice mail; set up your e-mail account and system.
- Visit with a few local experienced principals to set the stage for future collegial relations.
- Read the master contract of the school district to determine each bargaining unit's terms and conditions. If you have questions, consult with the superintendent or director of human resources for the district.

AFTER THE YEAR BEGINS

The temptation you will face as the school year begins is to settle in as the new principal and wait for some issues to come to you. That will certainly happen. However, you must persist in making a plan that will enable you to anticipate some major events and crises that you will face as a new principal. Some of these things will take place at the beginning of the school year and some will come later, but be prepared.

Building and Physical Plant Activities

- Keep an eye out for any unusual signs of wear and tear in the building, particularly as these might be related to the health and safety of students and staff.
- Carry out fire drills, tornado drills, and other forms of disaster drills as required by local laws and district policy.
- Make certain that custodial staff follow through on all assignments.
- Keep an eye on graffiti and vandalism around the school and make certain that, wherever possible, these problems are taken care of quickly; do not let your walls and property become a place where graffiti and tagging are acceptable.
- Make certain that hallway displays and bulletin boards are changed periodically throughout the year.
- Use the building as a symbol of openness and welcome to visitors from the community.

Instructional Management

- Depending on the size and type of school (elementary, middle, or high school) that you serve, determine the best way to meet with your teachers to share the insights that you (and your instructional improvement team or committee) have derived from a review of last year's achievement test data. Are there particular strengths seen in some areas and for some groups? What areas may need improvement? What strategies might be followed this year to achieve your instructional goals?

- Develop a tentative plan for staff development activities related to instructional improvement goals for the year. Discuss your tentative plan with your teachers.
- Be prepared for many parent visits soon after the school year begins. Although the purpose of these meetings will vary, rest assured that many sessions will be related to the desire to find different teachers than the ones now assigned to teach their children. While you may not wish to do so, make certain to take the time to listen to all concerns. At the same time, you need to have a mental checklist to use in making decisions regarding class transfers. Most requests might be denied, but there will be exceptions. Make sure that you think through such exceptions before your first parent visits.
- Have an informational meeting with parents early in the school year to explain testing dates and procedures that will be followed. Be prepared to indicate arrangements that have been (or will be) made for special tutoring sessions, Saturday classes, and other methods to help all children succeed with tests this year.
- The "good news" is that the first round of parent visits will begin to diminish at the beginning of the school year. The "bad news" is that your docket will remain full each day as discipline issues begin to replace parent concerns. Your work each day will never be completely predictable as long as you stay in the role of principal.
- Be prepared for the end of marking period (six weeks, nine weeks, etc.). These times will likely include many more parent visits, the need to talk to individual teachers, and the need to talk to students themselves. You should also review progress reports in the school as possible predictors of some difficulties that may appear later with regard to student performance on achievement tests.

Materials and Supplies

- Make certain that supplies ordered during the summer arrive and are distributed to your staff.
- Oversee the use of consumable supplies throughout the building (e.g., chalk, paper) to prevent an interruption of material in mid-year. Do not forget to consult with your custodial staff to ensure sufficient supplies of material to allow them to maintain the school as well.

Communications With Staff, Students, Parents, and Community

- Work with colleges and universities to identify appropriate placement procedures for student teachers and interns who will be working in your building throughout this next year.
- Establish and monitor appropriate parent and community volunteer programs.

- Review standing committee structures; establish new committees where needed to carry out important work in your school.
- Plan parent meeting dates for the year with your staff, PTA or PTO, booster clubs, and so on.
- On a continuing basis, make certain to communicate all important dates for the year with your staff.
- Follow all established dates and procedures related to teacher and staff evaluation.
- Get to know assistant principals (and also the informal leaders of your school) with whom you will be working; be particularly sensitive to the need to work with any assistant principals who might have been competitors for your job.
- Develop a clear roster of staff duties and special assignments.
- Work with local colleges and universities in the placement of student teachers and interns in your school.
- As time permits, visit as many classes as often as possible. (These visits may be "walk-through" evaluations or simply efforts to visit teachers and students informally. Either goal will have the positive effect of making you more visible in your school.)
- Review teacher lesson plans periodically, check on grading practices, and share with teachers your expectations regarding student performance. (This practice may seem new or may be "something we've never done around here before.")
- Learn the local culture as it relates to formal and informal holidays and events of the school. (For example, is Valentine's Day always a big day at your school? Do you have large numbers of teachers and students who observe certain religious holy days each year, thus increasing the likelihood that absentee rates will be high on some dates that are not listed as official holidays on your calendar? Does your district have a formal policy covering such days?)

System Responsibilities

- Learn the mandated census dates for your state (i.e., the official dates on which enrollment must be reported to the school district and the state educational agency).
- Work with appropriate district personnel to learn procedures associated with establishing your building budget for the next year. (You will likely have an absolute deadline for this material to be submitted to the central office; do not underestimate the amount of time that may be needed to carry out the task and meet the deadline.)
- Learn what is required and gather data systematically and continuously for the school's annual report that will have to be submitted to the central office at some point toward the end of the school year. (Again, this task is much simpler and more effective if you do not wait until the last minute to gather relevant data.)
- Systematically document your personal and professional accomplishments. (This will come into play when it is time for your performance appraisal and also in the future when you may be seeking a different position.)
- Develop a staffing plan for the following year. This should reflect such predictable events as the retirement of some of your teachers and the need to recruit replacements.

- As you get to know your teachers, it will become apparent very quickly who is very effective in the classroom while it will be equally clear which teachers are experiencing difficulty. Document all issues associated with ineffective professional performance of staff members if there is a need to proceed toward employment termination.
- Make certain to meet all deadlines for the completion of important tasks such as the evaluation of untenured teachers, first-year teachers, tenured faculty, and classified staff, and supervision of activities and athletic programs, planning for substitute teachers, and so on. Also comply with all stated procedures for reporting the results of the evaluations to all involved and concerned parties.

TOWARD THE END OF THE YEAR

The last few months and weeks of every school year are significant to your job, because many annual tasks pile up and you need to make sure that they are completed. Most important, the way in which you bring about closure to one school year often influences how successfully the next year will start. Do you remember all the things you discovered last summer and wished the previous principal had taken care of before you got there? Think what it would be like if you were the person who inherits your work from this year, and plan accordingly.

Building Maintenance

- Work with your district facilities manager and the head custodian in your building to identify major work and improvements that need to be done after the school year has concluded (e.g., roofing access ramps, window repairs, parking lot improvements, lighting).
- Establish a summer cleaning schedule with your custodial staff; include minor repairs and plans for storing and securing equipment and materials during the summer months.
- Check on instructional materials and other needed supplies for each grade level (elementary schools) or subject department (secondary schools) used throughout the building (e.g., replace teacher manuals, overhead transparencies, computer disks and CDs, and other similar items where needed).

Monitoring Achievement Tests

- Review policies regarding the monitoring of testing, collection of testing materials, and return of tests to offices established as test scoring centers.
- As soon as test scores are returned to the school, conduct a preliminary analysis of the strengths and limitations demonstrated by students who completed the exam.
- Work with the instructional leadership team to carry out a detailed analysis of all test scores, including the identification of specific performance for subgroups of the student population being tested. Begin to plan for goal setting for next year.
- Work with parents of students who were not successful in meeting the standards of the achievement test to identify future options.

- Present the overall findings of the achievement testing for the year to the entire faculty of the school. Test data should be disaggregated to enable teachers to appreciate areas of strength as well as weakness with regard to service to students.

Instructional Materials

- Learn how textbooks and other instructional materials distributed at the beginning of the school year are accounted for; are they to be stored in a central location or in individual classrooms?
- Survey teachers to determine additional instructional materials and equipment that may be needed next year.
- Collect from teachers grade books, lesson planning books, attendance records, and other materials that may be helpful to you when you are talking to parents, students, and central office administrators in the absence of teachers during the summer months. (In these days of increased reliance on technology for school record keeping, it may be that much of this information, particularly grades and attendance records, will be readily available for your review without collecting mounds of additional paper from teachers.)

Communication With Students, Parents, Teachers, and Staff

- Get ready for end-of-the-year award ceremonies by purchasing plaques, certificates, and trophies well in advance of the dates of the ceremonies.
- Distribute a survey to parents to determine their perceptions of the overall program effectiveness in the school.
- Distribute a survey to teachers to determine their perceptions of the quality of the school's programs. In addition, if you are comfortable with your staff and also with your sense of work as a principal, you may also wish to ask teachers to rate your performance during the school year. (You may also want to find out whether surveys like this have been done at your school. Also, consider carefully the messages that may be conveyed to your staff when the survey is administered. What are you going to do with the surveys? Or, will people think that this practice is all show, with no substance? Remember that teachers do not want their time wasted with meaningless activities.)
- Send thank you notes to your immediate supervisors, the district maintenance department, and others who have helped you survive this first year.
- Order and distribute special gifts (e.g., flowers, gift certificates) to parent volunteers.
- Sponsor a special social event (e.g., breakfast, tea) for parent volunteer groups, booster clubs, and so forth.
- Send an individual *handwritten* note of thanks to each teacher and staff member in your building. (Yes, even if you have a big building. And yes, even to teachers and staff members with whom you may have had some disagreements during the year.) A few hours of personal investment by you and a little writer's cramp will have a great payoff in the future. Be specific about the contributions that you appreciate and are rewarding.
- Inform teachers and staff members about summer workshops, seminars, and other professional enrichment opportunities sponsored by your district, the state department of education, the local business community, and so on.

- Sponsor thank you luncheons for your office and custodial staff.
- Submit your annual report to the central office.
- Share with staff members strategies or techniques that might be helpful in the improvement of school practices. This should be done in the spring so that staff will begin to plan for further discussion of these strategies next year.
- Alert staff to new districtwide programs and initiatives that may affect activities in individual schools next year. Again, sharing this information in the spring will make work in the fall much easier and productive.
- Lead the staff in discussions about possible concerns that will be addressed next year. (Clearly, this might include many conversations about how well the school did on achievement testing this year. However, there are likely to be many other issues that warrant consideration.) Formulate committees, encourage open dialogue during staff meetings, and plan ahead for staff inservice sessions that might be necessary next year.

General Management

- Plan the school's master schedule for next year.
- Provide room assignments for next year.
- Make sure that your local school policies are consistent with the distinction you want to promote for your educational program next year.
- Carry out student retention reviews for next year.
- Develop a tentative duty roster for next year.
- Review and set student activity fees for next year (and seek approval from your school board, if necessary).
- Plan and coordinate (and delegate direct responsibilities to others) such normal spring activities as the spring student play, prom, athletic banquets, sporting events, graduation ceremonies, and so on.
- Develop a tentative list of staff and faculty openings which may need to be filled during the summer.

I conclude this list of tasks that need to be done during different moments in your first year with three observations. First, this list is by no means exhaustive; it does not include all that you might need to do. Undoubtedly, you will find other activities in your own situation, and some of what is listed here may never be relevant in your case. Second, no priorities are suggested. It is not more important, for example, to send thank you notes to your district's custodial supervisor than it is to engage the staff in goal setting for the next year. You must make your own determination of what tasks must be done first. But it is a critical decision to make.

Third, and perhaps most important, is yet another understatement. *You cannot do it all!* While you begin your life as a principal willing to roll up your sleeves and dig into every aspect of your work with great enthusiasm and vigor, there simply aren't enough hours in a week for one person to attend to every aspect of each thing you will encounter, regardless of whether events and duties are planned or unplanned, formally mandated or informal. There is a way to reconcile this problem, however, and that is to make use of a word that we often hear but frequently forget: *Delegate!*

Before you start to cross off half the things that you are expected to do, there are a few important questions that you need to keep in mind. Remember that "delegating" is not simply a pleasant way of saying "dumping things on someone else because you don't want to mess with them." Nor does it mean that because you delegate duties you can automatically delegate responsibility. You are the principal, the boss, the person who will be held accountable (professionally as well as legally) for the proper performance of your job.

Here are a few questions to guide you and keep in mind as you consider the issue of delegating tasks and duties:

1. Who do you believe can be trusted to not only do a job, but do it well and competently?

2. Who might be able to do a task better than you can do it? (I know, this may bruise your ego, but there are things that others can do better than you!)

3. Who can you help by providing them with the opportunity to learn something from carrying out some duty? (Assistant principals, for example, need to learn how to review test data, too. And so do teachers who give evidence that they may some day become principals.)

4. Who can learn with you? There is so much to learn about school administration, and it is possible to learn about many things while others learn with you.

5. Who do you trust to follow through with an assignment without a lot of close supervision? (Remember, delegation should not turn out to be an exercise in micromanagement that requires you to look over someone's shoulder all day. Your secretary, for example, can no doubt do a lot to organize meetings of parent groups, community groups, and so forth.)

Delegating to others is often more easy to say than it is to do. As a newly-appointed principal in a new school, and perhaps a new school district, you will not know the people with whom you can work well enough to answer the previous questions without any problems. You will probably make some mistakes. Some people will disappoint you. Some who are chosen may not want to be chosen. These are risks that are worth taking, however. If you can begin to tap effectively into the vast resources of expertise, knowledge, and enthusiasm around you on a regular basis, you are well on your way to dropping the adjective "beginning" from your title of principal. And your school will be a better place because it is in the hands of a team of committed and caring educators.

BUILDING A PERSONAL PLAN

This chapter reviewed many of the important technical skills that a new school leader needs to master to become a proactive and effective leader. I suggested a large number of tasks as possible activities you may wish to carry out before the school year begins, after the year has started, and also in preparation for the closing of a school year. As you may have noted, a lot of things must be accomplished and I hope that you will not become overwhelmed with the enormous responsibilities of your job. This will be particularly true if you begin to make use of your ability to delegate some of your duties as the years continue. My goal here is to help you develop an understanding of major issues that need to be addressed in a systematic way. This type of proactive planning will assist you in becoming a true leader, not simply becoming a reactive manager of the next crises that are sure to walk into your office.

On these last few pages, consider your own situation and identify some important tasks that you will need to address throughout the next school year. Make certain to prioritize them. Although I have not yet discussed it, another issue that you will need to deal with in your principalship is effective time management. You will find numerous books, audiotapes, Web sites, and experts available for you to consult in this area, but really, time management means nothing more than making decisions about what must be attended to first. As a result, if you plan to attack several issues throughout the school year, begin here in the management of your time by asking, "What comes first?" After you decide the answer to that question, you may also want to identify specific strategies for carrying out your many duties according to a reasonable schedule. For example, if you plan to spend as much time in teachers' classrooms as possible during the year, it may be more helpful to be specific and say that you plan to visit each teacher's class at least three times each semester.

Before the Year Begins

_____

_____

_____

_____

After the School Year Is Under Way

_____

_____

_____

_____

In Preparation for the End of the School Year

_____

_____

_____

_____

In closing, remember that no matter how well you plan this next school year, you will encounter many surprises and unplanned events, or you may discover some responsibilities for which you do not feel well-prepared. In these cases, please remember that you will never be able to stand totally alone and be effective. Delegate to the many willing and capable people with whom you now work each day. Call other principals, seek advice from central office, and gather input from your teachers, secretarial and custodial staff, parents, and others. Remember that leading schools is a complex task, and complex tasks are generally tackled by a team.

SUGGESTED READING

Lovely, S. (2006). *Setting leadership priorities.* Thousand Oaks, CA: Corwin Press.

Ricken, R., Terc, M., & Ayres, I. (2006). *The elementary school principal's calendar* (2nd ed.). Thousand Oaks, CA: Corwin Press.

Ricken, R., & Terc, M. (2004). *The middle school principal's calendar.* Thousand Oaks, CA: Corwin Press.

Ricken, R., Simon, R., & Terc, M. (2000). *The high school principal's calendar.* Thousand Oaks, CA: Corwin Press.

Simon, R. A., & Newman, J. F. (2004). *Making time to lead.* Thousand Oaks, CA: Corwin Press.

5

Learning to Lead by Assisting

Stephanie Shinkunas had been a teacher in the Amber City Schools for eight years when she decided to enroll in the master's degree and school administration certification programs at Central Tech University. After two years of part-time study and what seemed like about a million miles of driving between her home, school, and the university, Stephanie finally completed her degree. Last March she was ready to start looking for her first job as a school administrator.

Stephanie was really pleased to be offered what she considered to be an almost perfect job. The Amber City Schools offered her the position of assistant principal at Clarence Crenshaw Middle School, one of the newer buildings in the district, which was only a mile from Stephanie's home. She knew the neighborhood, many of the families associated with the school, and quite a few of the students. More important, she was going to be working with Dr. Carol Spencer, one of the most respected principals in the school district. Carol had a reputation for being very demanding of her assistants, but every one of them had become a principal after only a few years of work with her. She definitely appeared to be the kind of mentor that Stephanie wanted in her first administrative position.

True to form, the first few meetings between the principal and her new assistant were very formal. Carol spent about 30 minutes on each of three occasions outlining very specifically what she expected of Stephanie. She noted everything from how she expected her assistant to be dressed, to how they were to behave when interacting with teachers, to what time she expected Stephanie to arrive at school each morning. They also carefully reviewed the district job description for assistant principals, line by line. Carol emphasized that Stephanie would be called upon to do everything the district required, and there would be many times when the catchall phrase "all other duties assigned by the principal" would be exercised. Although she was a bit overwhelmed at first, Stephanie was still eager to learn by working next to an expert principal.

As the year progressed, however, Stephanie became increasingly frustrated in her new job. For one thing, she felt as if she were little more than Carol's gofer on many days. Often, she thought that she was being set up by having to stay in her office for most days while Carol left the building to attend principals' meetings, speak to community groups, or serve on yet another committee for the school district. She spent a lot of time greeting parents who wanted to know about the school's programs. Stephanie had hoped that she could do a lot of other things that were much more enjoyable than simply handling the walk-in parents who often came to the school to drop off forgotten books for their children, ask questions about meetings or school activities, or to complain about teachers or school board policies. In addition, she quickly realized that Carol was doing a number of things that she did not support. As a person out of the classroom for only a few months, Stephanie often felt she was more comfortable in the teachers' lounge than she was in the administrative offices with Carol.

"I don't think this is going to work out. I'll never become a principal of my own school at this rate," Stephanie confided to Charlie Wise. Charlie, now the director of pupil services for Amber City, had been a well-respected assistant principal and principal for several years before taking his current central office job. He also had become a mentor for several of the beginning administrators in the district, including Stephanie, who had once been one of Charlie's teachers.

"So you don't like doing all the junk work while Carol takes the glamour duty. Is that what's bothering you?" Stephanie didn't really want to admit it, but Charlie had really captured what she was thinking. "Learn how to do the little things. They'll become bigger later. And while I'm on my soapbox, don't fall into the temptation of siding with the teachers or anyone else to undercut your boss. Remember, you're an assistant principal." Stephanie didn't really like it, but because she respected Charlie so much, she decided to follow his advice for the remainder of at least her first year.

If you're at a high school, middle school, or junior high school, chances are very good that you got to where you are now serving as an assistant principal for a few years. If you're an elementary school principal, you may or may not have worked as an assistant. If you didn't, that may be quite unfortunate. Serving as an assistant principal, although typically not a glamorous or prestigious job in many school systems, might be one of the most powerful learning experiences you can have as you prepare to become an effective principal. Chapters 3, 4, and 5 of this book address ways in which you can develop greater confidence and competence in the performance of technical duties attached to the role of the principal. Serving as an assistant principal for a few years can be an extremely powerful way to become better prepared to do the next job you wish to attain in education.

In this chapter, some practical tips are offered to anyone who might now be serving in the role of assistant principal with an eye toward taking a principalship in the future.

REMEMBER YOUR ROLE

The role of assistant principal can be a very difficult one to carry out effectively. On the one hand, you are no longer a classroom teacher. Presumably, you made a deliberate choice to move into a career in school administration. That is why you enrolled in graduate courses at a university or participated in some similar form of school management training. You probably spent a lot of time and money pursuing your goal to be an educational leader. In most states, you had to go through the same pre-service preparation required of principals. You may know colleagues who were able to go directly from the classroom into the principal's office.

On the other hand, if you are an assistant principal, you are clearly not in the inner circle of being a principal. You are no longer a teacher, but when principals' meetings are held, you are typically the person who is expected to stay at your school and run the building while the principal is out. In this case, you will be defining yourself largely as an "assistant to the principal." You may see the assistant principalship as a regular and desirable step in the long-term process of becoming a principal. You must serve as an assistant principal but, at the same time, use your time wisely to cultivate the skills that can eventually be put to use when you have your own building.

USING THE ROLE FOR THE FUTURE

You may wish to remember several things if your goal is to move into a principalship after serving as an assistant.

Cool Your Ego

No doubt, you are a capable, bright, energetic, and obviously ambitious educator. Suddenly you are an assistant principal, and you now find yourself in a job in which you get some of the worst and dirtiest duties imaginable as a school administrator. You are the person who listens to complaints. You deal with most of the discipline problems in your school. In many ways, you are a bit like a triage nurse in a hospital emergency room who must decide if the nature of the "injury" is sufficiently severe to bring it forward immediately to a doctor or, in this case, the principal. Also, you are often the person who is assigned the task of contacting parents about problems with their child's behavior, attendance, test scores, or many other issues that are really quite important but nonetheless unpleasant. While you do these kinds of things, your principal gets to stand in front of everyone and take credit for all the good things that happen in your school—even though you, the teachers, and the staff may have done all the work. But the boss gets all the credit and praise.

Probably every current or former assistant principal has at some time or another held thoughts quite similar to those in the previous paragraph. In some ways, the feelings might be a bit exaggerated. In other cases, however, the scenario presented above might be completely accurate: You do the work while someone else gets the credit.

This is when the temptation to begin feeling like a victim, or feeling sorry for yourself, is something that really needs to be avoided. The position that you hold is that of assistant principal. You are not the co-principal of your school. Although this obvious statement may shock you at first, remember that you were not hired to be the lead administrator. Rather, your job is defined pretty clearly as a person who will assist the lead administrator. This means, perhaps more than anything else, that you may need to rein in your understandable pride and ego. Again, you were hired because you demonstrated more promise for leadership and management skills than others who applied for your position—didn't you?

The fact is that you were most likely hired because you appeared to have the potential to add your skills to what is already present in your school. In short, you were probably selected, at least to some degree, because people assumed you could work effectively with the principal.

In the space below, indicate some ways in which you might face potential conflicts between your own need to be recognized and the needs of your principal.

_____

_____

_____

_____

Indicate some ways in which you might work to resolve these potential conflicts between your ego and your principal.

_____

_____

_____

_____

Assist the Principal

Your job, quite frankly, is to assist your principal. One of the most important ways to provide that support is by doing everything that you can to make your principal look good and achieve success. What that means, again, is that you have to learn to live with the fact that you will need to suppress what is a natural desire to call attention to your own abilities and accomplishments and instead remain in the shadows.

A couple of things may happen. If you are fortunate to be working with an extremely capable and effective principal, he or she will no doubt recognize that you have been quietly and patiently sitting in the wings. For the most part, appreciation may not be shown immediately or even extremely visibly. But a good principal is more than likely able to discern competence and a job well done. In the majority of cases, remember that your good principal was probably a good assistant principal at one time.

However, you may be assisting a person who is less than effective. In short, you may be working with the worst principal in the district. Continue to be supportive and do everything that you can to make him or her look good. It's frustrating and it's hard work, but you should remember two things. First, if you do a good job of covering for an ineffective principal, you will do what can be done to help your school—to help the teachers, and most critically, students. It's not their fault that they are working in a place where leadership is not strong. Second, if you are able to realize the ineffectiveness of your principal, it's probably not a major secret unknown to other principals, the superintendent, central office, school board members, and most everyone in the community at large. If you do your job and make things work for your boss, people will recognize who is doing the job.

If you take the attitude that because you're stuck with an ineffective principal you don't have to work very hard, something else will likely happen. If you don't provide leadership and do the job that the principal should be doing, your school will likely look quite poor to those who look at its performance. You will be a part of the ineffective administration at a failing school, and your reputation and career could easily suffer. Remember that, in many cases, you may not get the kudos that come along with good things that may happen in your school. However, you can rest assured that if your school appears to be failing, you will be blamed along with the principal. People paint with very broad brushes.

What are some of the ways in which you can increase your status by helping your principal succeed?

_____

_____

_____

_____

Keep Quiet

Whether you are blessed by working with a great principal or forced to work with someone less capable, remember that you always owe your boss discretion and loyalty. A big part of those qualities is defined by learning not to bad-mouth your boss, gossip, leak information to others, or above all, disagree with your boss in public. As a school administrator, you will have access to many things that must be kept confidential. By the same token, you will make your job and the job of your principal much more difficult by speaking about your boss behind his or her back. It will be a temptation—if you are drawn into conversations with teachers, other administrators, parents, or community members—to say things that might be taken as critical of the principal's work. The old saying that if others hear you speaking ill of someone, they will begin to wonder whether you speak ill of them in their absence is one that is worth thinking about.

You may find legitimate situations in which it will be necessary to disagree with something said or done by the principal. Two words of advice are offered. First, if you disagree with something, say it directly to the principal, not to half the teachers in your school. Second, say it behind closed doors. The best analogy here might be that disagreements between colleagues, as between spouses, should not be done "in front of the kids." To do so can easily encourage those who might seek opportunities for dissension to divide and conquer. No one is asking that you park your brain on the curb outside your school each day. You need not become a sycophant or "yes person" who defers to the wishes of your principal at all times. However, when you disagree with something that your boss says or does, you have a responsibility to decide whether it is of such consequence that you must bring it up, and if you do, to remain discreet and courteous by discussing it in private.

Remember that the business of operating a school is one that should be guided primarily by engaging in activities that are directly related to the learning needs of students. Having a situation in which disagreement occurs between members of the management or leadership team causes turmoil in the school. It disrupts faculty morale and is anything but a good situation for anyone. For the students in a school in which such situations exist, it is like having constant bickering between parents in an unhappy home.

If you were to spend time with your principal (in a private session) and discuss some of the ways in which you might disagree with some of the things that he or she has asked you to do, what might you say?

_____

_____

_____

_____

Now that you have listed these things, it is up to you to decide whether it is wise to share these concerns with the person with whom you now work.

Listen, Listen . . . Then Listen Some More

The great advantage of adopting a stance in which you keep your mouth shut and cool your ego is that you are likely to learn a lot of things very quickly. You can do this through a very simple learning technique that you have no doubt shared with hundreds of students enrolled in your classes over the years. The technique is simply to listen and absorb.

One of the realities of being an assistant principal in your first formal job in school administration is that people likely realize that you do not have a great deal of prior managerial experience. Although you may find yourself in situations where you feel as if you must act and take a strong stance because, after all, you are now an administrator, keep in mind the old saying that good decisions are often those not made—at least not immediately.

A constant temptation for those who are new to administration is to demonstrate their skills and strengths by taking immediate, decisive action on everything that comes across their desks. It is almost an unwritten set of instructions that exists somewhere that says, "You are weak (and a bad administrator) if you put off any decision." It is true that many in your organization will press you for a quick answer for every issue. And those same people will be your strongest allies—if you consistently decide issues to their liking. It is remarkable how "good" administrators frequently become very "bad" overnight, based on the strength of making only one contrary decision!

I am not suggesting that not making any decisions is good practice. Too often, schools suffer from a type of organizational paralysis that comes from decision avoidance by superintendents, school boards, principals, or others. But absolute, unyielding, and often rash decisions are equally unproductive, too. Two things are useful to remember to help you decide the proper balance between paralysis and authoritarianism.

First, as an assistant principal, you have not only the opportunity but the duty to defer many of your most challenging decisions to a higher authority, namely, your principal.

That leads to the second recommendation for learning about effective decision making by listening. One of the reasons your principal has the job he or she does is normally because of greater experience as an administrator. That probably means that even when you don't agree with some stances taken by your boss, it is likely that they have some foundation in past practice. And the only way you are likely to achieve that same degree of experience is by remaining open to the thoughts of others and listening. And observing. And asking questions so you can listen some more. The key here is to adopt an attitude of willingness to learn by absorbing as much as possible.

Of course, the idea of listening as much as possible needs to be tempered a bit by your need to learn as you absorb what others do. I am not suggesting that you should never question the reasons and assumptions made by your principal. In fact, asking the question, "Why did you take such and such a stance?" from time to time may be helpful to you and also the principal. Too often, experienced administrators make so many decisions on the basis of past experiences that they almost lose track of why they are doing what they are doing. In some cases, a periodic "Why?" from a colleague can be an important tool to promote greater reflection and more effective performance.

List some of the ways in which you have already learned more about being an effective leader by listening to and absorbing from more experienced colleagues with whom you now work.

_____

_____

_____

_____

Ask to Do More

A common problem for those who serve as assistant principals is that they often get typecast in their roles. If your first administrative post is serving as the assistant principal in charge of discipline and attendance and you do a great job, you may have a problem. Forevermore, you may develop a well-deserved reputation as an outstanding disciplinarian. That is certainly not a negative statement. However, if your goal is to eventually move into a principalship of your own, being locked in as a disciplinarian—and nothing else—is likely to prevent others from seeing all the other things you can do. Providing fair and effective discipline is important, but a good principal (and good principal candidates) needs to do much more. Financial management and budgeting, staff development, community relations, instructional improvement, and so many other responsibilities make up the life of a modern principal. If school districts do not perceive that you have the skills and experience in these other areas of administration, you may be an assistant principal for quite some time.

It is absolutely essential, therefore, that you work to develop skills and expertise in as many areas of campus management as you can while you serve as an assistant principal. If you are the only assistant in the school, it may be somewhat easier to gain experience in a fairly wide range of areas of service. But, if you are part of a larger team of assistant principals and your colleagues have already been assigned specific areas of coverage (curriculum, student activities, community relations, and so on), your task of broadening your portfolio becomes much more complex. Remember it is likely that some, if not all, of your colleagues have become bored with the areas in which they work. Not everyone necessarily wants to diversify in the way you might. But you will need to increase your personal awareness of issues and concerns encountered in many different functional areas of operating a school.

How can this happen? The first step should probably involve a frank conversation with your principal. Even though you have been hired essentially to do the job of assisting a principal, it is not likely to surprise your boss that you have ambitions and that some day you will want your own school. Explain what may be quite obvious. You need to gain insights into many different areas of school improvement and leadership.

Talking to your principal about trying to find ways to involve you in different administrative responsibilities may not pay off. After all, it may be that you are the only assistant in the school and the principal prefers to do certain things (e.g., curriculum and staff development). It is unlikely that you will be able to "diversify" in your present school. If that is the case, you may wish to think about seeking a transfer to a different assignment. Many may question the wisdom of this advice. Traditionally, there has been a view that lateral transfers are negative; don't go somewhere else to do the same job. But in this case, the suggestion may be to seek a similar job title but with different responsibilities.

Stay Alive Professionally

If you are now an assistant principal, you will no doubt find amusing the observation that you are very busy with your job. Simply keeping your head above water and handling all the duties of your job is quite a task. But if you want to be a principal in the foreseeable future, you may need to do even more. For example, you cannot neglect the need to stay tuned to professional issues, recent research, and other developments in the field of education and educational research. To state the obvious, pursuing a personal professional development agenda is not always consistent with the time demands of serving as a school administrator, particularly the assistant principal, who is so often at the mercy of "all other duties assigned."

Despite the limitations of time (and energy), two areas are recommended for personal growth while you strive to refine your leadership skills. One is reading and the other is participating in professional seminars, meetings, and conferences.

Engaging in a reading agenda is a relatively simple activity, although going home to read a book after a hard day at a school in which you serve as an assistant principal is not something you would necessarily put high on your personal priority list. However, if you are going to keep current in professional practice trends, the best way to do so is to keep up with recent literature, either in the form of journal articles or with selected books. You cannot possibly become an expert in everything presented in the educational literature, but you may carve out an area in which you do most of your reading. For example, some school administrators read almost exclusively the work of William Glaser and his vision of the "Quality School." Others may follow the writing and research of Carl Glickman and his work in "Developmental

Supervision." Neither of these authors will write about every single topic that needs to be addressed by effective school administrators. But Glaser, Glickman, and many other serious educational writers offer broad visions of effective schooling that are worthy of review, reflection, and perhaps adoption. The key here is that I am not suggesting any single author or series of work but rather encouraging you to keep your mind alive and well so that it can be used as a valuable resource of knowledge to improve both present and future administrative practice.

In the space below, indicate any recent books or other material you have read (or plan to read in the near future). Indicate what appears relevant to you about being an assistant principal.

_____

_____

_____

_____

The second recommended practice to help assistant principals remain alive professionally involves participation in seminars and conferences. To a large extent, your ability to follow through with this suggestion is dependent on resources and the goodwill and permission of your principal. On the other hand, even if it might mean using your own finances and spending vacation periods, personal days, or weekends to attend professional meetings, think about doing so for at least two reasons. First, you are likely to learn some important things about topics that may be important to your work both now and in the future. Second, attending professional meetings will put you in contact with many other people who will, in turn, get to know you and your abilities. That form of self-marketing through personal networks will have considerable value when you begin looking around for a principalship some day.

Indicate any professional conferences, meetings, or seminars in which you have recently participated. Indicate some of the benefits you believe you have acquired through your involvement.

_____

_____

_____

_____

What professional events would you like to attend during the next year or two? Why?

_____

_____

_____

_____

In a later chapter, I will offer a number of additional suggestions for your professional development. The critical thing to remember, regardless of what approaches you may follow, is that if your goal is to grow into a principalship some day, you need to continue to grow professionally.

Stay Positive

The last recommendation offered to you as an assistant principal may be the single most powerful one because it touches all other items listed. Be as positive and enthusiastic as you can about yourself, your job, your colleagues, your students, and your school district. This is not always an easy thing to do, of course. As an administrator, a big part of your life automatically involves being "knee deep in alligators." It is more than a little tempting to spend a lot of time feeling bad about your job as an assistant principal. After all, since you do a lot of discipline work, you see a lot of students who are in trouble. At least in part as a result of that, you encounter many parents who are not happy. Because you work as an assistant, you often get many less-than-glamorous jobs to do for your boss. And as an insider, you often get to see and understand many of the biggest problems faced by your district. In short, it's easy to become cynical and begin looking only at the worst features of life as an educator.

Now, stop and think about what dwelling on the problems only may do for you as you begin to build a career as an educational leader. Imagine that you are involved with searching for a new principal for a school. Also, think of what reaction you would likely have to an applicant for the position if he or she spent a good deal of time criticizing or complaining about his or her present school or district. Compare your impressions of that person with someone who had a reputation for being positive, enthusiastic, and a booster for his or her present situation. Given those two alternatives as applicants, if equally qualified for the principalship, most (if not all) school systems will select the person who is positive.

Building an image as someone who is enthusiastic and happy cannot take place only during the few weeks in which you might be an applicant for a job, of course. A reputation as a team player who can make a positive contribution as a principal gets built over a long period of time and, as a result, depends on many things. One of the critical things that you need to remember is that you are on stage during your entire career. Whether you know it or not, people are looking at you as a potential candidate for future positions. As soon as it is clear that a principal of a school is retiring, being transferred, or leaving for whatever reason, people begin to think of possible candidates as replacements. You want to be on that list. The way to do that is to be visible and perceived as a person who would be a positive addition to a school. The best way to be excluded from further consideration as an administrator in your district is to get a reputation as a person who complains, whines, and has poor "people skills" when working with others in the school, district, or community.

When you are at meetings with people from other schools, it is critical that you be a cheerleader for your present principal, school, and district. No matter what others may say or believe about your current situation, it is critical that your public stance be one of support and commitment to the best place you can possibly be—at least for now. Taking any other stance creates an image that you do not want. You do not want anyone to fear what you do or might do or say about their school if you become their principal. If you are to be the leader of "our school," people want to believe that you will support them as much as you do in your present situation.

Regardless of any problems that might exist in your present school or district, list ten or more features of your present situation that make it a good place to work.

_____

_____

_____

_____

Make a copy of your list and read it over each time you head out your door. Do not do a similar list of problems and shortcomings. Frankly, no one really cares about these things or wants to hear your gripes or problems you are having back home. Everyone has their own concerns.

Stay positive, be enthusiastic, and project an image that allows people to have confidence that you will be the same kind of person in your next job.

YOUR PERSONAL PLAN

If you are currently an assistant principal who wishes to become a principal in the near future, review the suggested learning strategies presented in this chapter. Identify those issues that you believe are most relevant to you, and indicate what you plan to do during the next year or two. For example, you might wish to identify a few books that you would like to read as a way to stay alive professionally.

_____

_____

_____

_____

If you are not currently an administrator but you are planning to start your career as an assistant principal, you may wish to identify which of the listed strategies are issues that you plan to address so that service as an assistant principal can be a powerful approach to your formation as an educational leader.

SUGGESTED READING

Daresh, J. (2004). *Beginning the assistant principalship: A practical guide for new school administrators.* Thousand Oaks, CA: Corwin Press.

Glanz, J. (2004). *The assistant principal's handbook: Strategies for success.* Thousand Oaks, CA: Corwin Press.

Weller, L. D., & Weller, S. (2002). *The assistant principal: Essentials for effective school leadership.* Thousand Oaks, CA: Corwin Press.

6

Assuming Responsibility for Accountability

Cyrus Castle had been regarded by most residents of the town of Antwhistle as one of the best school principals in the history of the local school district. Since this is a small town, virtually every resident had some type of encounter—positive or negative—with "Mr. C." while going through school. And even those who had unpleasant recollections of Mr. C. and his "board of education" applied to their backside as a form of discipline had fond recollections of his smile, jokes, and general contributions to many local charities and causes. In short, Cyrus was a genuine local hero and a tradition in town.

It was not a great surprise when the superintendent called him after his retirement in the spring to ask him if he would consent to serve the district again, this time as a mentor to the three newly hired school administrators that had come on board after Cyrus's retirement and the construction of two new elementary schools. They were constructed to serve the new housing development that now serves "Antwhistle Willows," a subdivision that was attracting many residents who no longer wanted to deal with the city life of nearby communities. Cyrus was most pleased to accept the superintendent's invitation to work with Maria Sanchez, Eli McGuffey, and Arthur Caine, the new principals. None had any formal past experience as school administrators, although Eli had been an at-risk coordinator at the Antwhistle Junior High School for three years. Maria and Arthur were both newcomers to the area. They had prior successful careers as classroom teachers; Maria had worked in nearby Carson Grove, while Arthur came from a large school system up near the state capital.

Cyrus spent the summer before the new school year planning for his work as a mentor to the three rookies. He was quite happy with the thought that he could help newcomers to the profession he loved for so long get off to a positive start. Like many who serve as mentors to new administrators, Mr. C. saw his service as a way to pay back good things to his school and community and also continue to be a teacher.

About two weeks before the school year began, Cyrus arranged a meeting with the three beginning principals. They met early one morning for breakfast at Rosie's, a local institution "serving hungry Antwhistlers for the past 47 years."

After breakfast was over, it was time for the business portion of the small group meeting. All three new principals began their discussion by thanking Cyrus for agreeing to assist them this first year. They knew that the local hero would be doing this for no pay, and since none of them had the advantage of time served as an assistant principal, there would likely be many cases where phone calls to Cyrus would be frantic and necessary.

Cyrus began his comments with a lengthy description of how he really looked forward to working with his young colleagues. He truly had loved his time at Antwhistle Elementary School, but now he was looking forward to a bit of "R and R" with Cornelia, his wife of 42 years, and Rusty, his German shepherd. They had a lot of fishing and hunting to catch up with, and they were looking forward to breaking in the new travel trailer by visiting Civil War battlegrounds in some of the surrounding states. He shared with the group some large blocks of time when the Castle family would be incommunicado. But he noted that things would be just fine since he knew that all three of his new colleagues had the "right stuff"—otherwise they would never have been hired in a great district such as Antwhistle.

Cyrus then proceeded to share a number of "war stories" about his days as a principal in town. He rattled off the names of many local citizens who had "moments of greatness" in his school. He also mentioned that Roscoe Spencer, now the state representative for the area, was a former student who met the Castle "board of education" on several occasions. The new principals smiled and enjoyed the conversation, but all started to get a bit concerned when Cyrus distributed copies of his "Rules for Success" to them. Among the several items on the list were statements such as

- Above all, keep the grass in front of your school mowed and watered. People want to be proud of their nice school!
- Go to as many church and community events in town as possible. Parents want their principal to be seen, approachable, and dedicated to the community.
- If you're not a golfer now, take lessons soon. The leaders of the community judge people by their sportsmanship.
- Don't drink anything stronger than coffee, water, or soft drinks out in public within at least 25 miles of town.
- Be very careful about your public demeanor out in the community. More than one school administrator has lost a job because of an indiscretion.
- Although the use of the Castle board of education is no longer permitted in schools, remain firm in your approach to discipline. New teachers shouldn't smile before Christmas, but new principals need to wait until next summer's Fourth of July parade.

When the new principals had a chance to read the list, there was a silence in the room. "Well, what do you think? Any questions before I get Cornelia and Rusty and drive off to Gettysburg?" asked Cyrus.

"Mr. Castle, these are some great tips here, but you haven't had much to say about the state accountability mandates for public schools, annual testing, and the No Child Left Behind legislation from Washington. How did you deal with that?" asked Martha, with Arthur and Eli nodding in agreement with the gist of her question.

"I had a perfect solution for all that nonsense," laughed Cyrus. "That was the reason for buying the motor home and announcing my retirement. The fact is, I truly believe in the motto, 'This too shall pass.' I've seen this kind of nonsense coming from politicians for many years. It will go away with the next round of elections."

"But what has been done to get the students, parents, and teachers ready for testing every year? How have the students in Antwhistle been doing on the tests?" asked Eli.

"Just fine. Most of our kids come from good homes where parents read to their kids, keep playing on computers to a minimum, support their schools, and show respect for teachers. Kids here come ready to learn, so testing is not going to be the same big deal as it may have been in communities like you and Maria came from, Eli," responded the mentor principal. "Just trust me. Mow your lawns, don't drink or smoke, play some golf, but don't smile too much. You'll all do fine. Give me a call whenever I can help, and have a great year!"

Cyrus clearly had given them everything he planned to share in this session. He paid the breakfast bill, shook everyone's hand, and headed toward the door. The three new principals sat quietly for a few moments. Finally, Maria turned to Eli and said, sadly, "What a nice man. It must have been great where he used to work!"

The principalship is no longer the job it used to be. Not too many years ago, doing a good job as a campus administrator meant "keeping the lid on things" at a school. Keep the teachers in line, make sure the school looks nice, pat a few backs here and there to maintain political ties in the community, and above all, discipline the students. To be sure, there have always been periodic reviews of the curriculum by groups like the state education agency or regional accreditation organizations to make certain that students were learning and that something of value was being taught. But, in the words of principals like Cyrus Castle, "Keeping the lawn mowed out in front of the school makes people believe that there is a good school inside."

The last ten years or so have truly become a new age in schools, namely, the "Age of Accountability." The days that Cyrus remembered are long gone. There is much more to being the administrator of schools than there was in the past. Regardless of the reasons, the United States has witnessed an increase in interest in ensuring that schools are, indeed, providing adequate educational programs to all students (a requirement found in the constitutions of all states). Whether caused by parental concern, educator frustration, or even political posturing (as suggested by the retired principal in the opening scenario), steps have been enacted in all states and at the federal level to support the mandate of quality education across the United States. In general, educators have no problems with the intent of these measures. Difficulties often occur with the methods used to assure all that effective education is taking place.

Perhaps the single most powerful model of the expectation that schools and school districts would be held accountable for student learning is found in the terms of federal legislation. The federal reauthorization of the Elementary and Secondary Education Act of 1965 was presented and supported as law during the first administration of President George W. Bush in 2003. This legislation, the No Child Left Behind Act (NCLB), has been either praised or cursed nationally as the source of most current measures associated with efforts to reform education in public schools across the nation. It includes many specific requirements for schools to ensure that all children, regardless of race, ethnicity, or economic level, are able to achieve adequate education at taxpayers' expense. The legislation has its roots in the perceptions held by many concerning the overall adequacy of schooling in recent years. Among these are the public belief that students are not generally sufficiently prepared in the basic skill areas of reading, writing, and mathematics; that American public school students are lagging behind students in other nations of the world in key areas such as science, mathematics, and foreign language learning; that the consequences of these inadequacies are likely to have a continuing negative impact on America's ability to compete economically with other industrialized nations of the world; and above all, practices and problems in America's public schools are unevenly felt by students in different ethnic, racial, gender, and socioeconomic groups. In short, NCLB supporters take the stance that while all children in the United States have access to free public education, the quality of that education has varied significantly from state to state, community to community, and societal subgroup to subgroup over the years. The goal of NCLB is to bring about equality of educational opportunity for all children and ensure that Hispanic children in South Texas, African American students in the inner cities of Detroit and Cleveland, and boys and girls in wealthy North Shore suburbs near Chicago all have a chance to succeed because of quality schooling.

In what other ways do you believe that legislation at the national level such as NCLB and actions taken at the state level have the potential to improve the quality of education in the United States?

_____

_____

_____

_____

The adoption of mandated programs and practices such as NCLB is, of course, not without criticism as well. While few would dispute the goals of enhancing overall quality and the effort to equalize the quality of education by making certain that basic standards of educational achievement can be realized by all children, there are, nonetheless, arguments that question current accountability movements. Some of the issues frequently raised by critics are based on the following observations:

1. The status of poor programs of public education in America has been greatly overstated by many. While problems exist, the vast majority of schools in this country are and have been focused on providing quality education to all students for many years.

2. Frequent efforts to discredit American schools because they are not comparable to schools in Germany, Japan, and many other countries of the world are distortions of reality, in large part because the goals and social expectations

of schools in countries around the world differ so greatly. For example, Americans want their children to learn how to read and write. But we also value students who are well-adjusted to social expectations and well-rounded in terms of involvement in athletics and other activities. We also want our children to participate in afterschool work experiences, athletics, and social events. All of these issues are rarely a part of the "schooling" experience in other nations of the world.

3. Assuming that children are not learning because test scores are low is an inaccurate assumption that overlooks the limitations of standardized testing to gauge much more than test-taking ability.

4. Current legislation places too much emphasis on testing of children, a practice that defines learning in narrow terms because the curricula of schools, districts, and states becomes defined in terms of "what is needed to score well on the tests." As a result, we "teach to the test" so much that we ignore the opportunity for children to learn by "thinking outside the box" and develop creativity. Some have even gone so far as describing the national reform effort as nothing but "No Child's Behind Left Untested."

5. From a practical point of view, NCLB legislation is yet another example of an "unfunded mandate" of government; it makes costly requirements of school districts across the nation without providing sufficient financial support for schools to implement what is required. For example, if pupils are unable to pass tests at grade levels, and they are retained for one (or more) years at their current grades, school districts could face the need to build more facilities and hire a large number of new teachers to serve the influx of retained students. In a school system with 5,000 students at Grade 3, for example, 90 percent of pupils might pass, and 10 percent (500 pupils) would be retained, thus potentially creating the need for a school that could house 500 students. If that type of result is projected over several grade levels in a school district, the obvious implications would result in colossal expenditures for new buildings.

6. The definition of accountability and achievement is too narrowly focused. If students do not perform well on standardized tests each year, the implication of current policy is that educators (teachers, principals, counselors, superintendents, and so forth) are somehow incompetent and deserving of all blame. Totally absent from the legislation is emphasis on parental responsibility and individual student accountability for their personal learning.

7. Terms in NCLB are often vague and apparently insensitive to social realities at times. Perhaps the best example of vagueness is found in the expectation for "Adequate Yearly Progress" (AYP) to be demonstrated by all students. While the notion that children should learn a reasonable amount of content knowledge and acquire sufficient skills each year in a school makes sense, the terms of NCLB are not that simple. Instead, an often confusing array of indicators and expectations, as noted later in this chapter, often obscure what this relatively simple and important concept may involve. School administrators often complain that AYP is used to punish schools rather than as a means of measuring true student progress from year to year. In terms of NCLB standards that appear contradictory to reality, there is the expectation that schools would hire nothing but "highly qualified teachers." Most would agree

that schools should insist on finding teachers who know their subject areas and demonstrate a commitment to serving children. However, the reality that needs to be recognized is that teaching is not a profession that is very attractive to many these days. Salary levels, opportunities for career advancement, working conditions (which may relate to the expectations of NCLB itself), fringe benefits, and other factors are now increasingly identified as strong disincentives to individuals who might otherwise follow careers as "highly qualified teachers." In response to this reality, many states have initiated programs to enable individuals who appear "highly qualified" in terms of subject area expertise to move quickly into teaching roles through alternative teacher certification programs. While this strategy may enable greater numbers of people who know subject matter (e.g., in math and science because they used to work in fields where these skills were needed by employees) to suddenly achieve instant "highly qualified teacher" status, these individuals are often drawn from the ranks of unemployed workers in other fields who see teaching as a "backup job" without strong commitment to serving children as a major focus of their work. Principals often report significant concerns with alternative certification program (ACP) teachers because there is often a lack of understanding and appreciation of student needs, interests, and other conditions that promote true learning.

8. The tone of NCLB is largely punitive. In the name of making public education more accountable to taxpayers' assumptions that children entrusted to local schools would learn basic skills each year, provisions of NCLB suggest that if the standards laid out are not met, drastic measures are warranted to punish schools for failing to meet public expectations. These include the threat of losing large numbers of students who would transfer to "better" schools, the loss of financial support, and ultimately, closure. Critics point to the fact that, in many cases, schools with "failing grades" serve communities with low expectations for educational success and parents and children who have no interest in achieving success in schools in the first place. Rather than operating under the suggestion that "the school is bad and should be closed," some schools should be provided with additional resources to enable the development of more effective programs and practices to reach out to populations of children who need stronger intervention, not simply "market choice" to "take their business elsewhere."

TERMS OF THE NO CHILD LEFT BEHIND ACT

As noted earlier, No Child Left Behind legislation holds certain expectations for school performance and the ability to meet key objectives in the areas of accountability, average yearly progress, and the recruitment and selection of qualified classroom teachers.

Accountability

Perhaps the first term that needs to be understood is the word "accountability" as it is used in the legislation. This is, after all, the cornerstone of everything that is promised in both the national policy of NCLB and parallel programs developed in each state. In its analysis of NCLB, the national principals' associations collaborated with the Educational Research Service to produce a useful document that should be a resource for every principal, whether a beginner or seasoned veteran. This work, *The K-12 Principal's Guide to No Child Left Behind* (McLeod, D'Amico, & Protheroe, 2003) provides the following "Characteristics of Good Accountability Systems."

A good accountability system must

1. set ambitious, but realistic goals for improvement in student achievement;

2. measure improvement for students and schools against state-defined academic standards;

3. hold schools and districts accountable for raising student achievement, including the achievement of low income and minority students, on a specific timeline with benchmarks;

4. require continuous improvement for all schools and for all groups within schools to close the achievement gap;

5. be statewide, transparent, and understandable to parents and other stakeholders;

6. minimize opportunities to "game" the system;

7. ensure that all students participate in assessments;

8. include as determinative indicators of school progress only quantifiable student outcomes;

9. be structurally sound to ensure true reform; and,

10. reward success and ensure that students are provided with effective remedies, including public school options, in case of persistent failures. (p. 72)

These characteristics of accountability make it clear that being a school principal today and in the foreseeable future will not allow beginning principals or experienced principals to carry on with "business as usual." Based on the previous list that defines accountability, the following seem to be issues that you will need to address:

- Principals will need to become directly involved with the business of overseeing teachers who may no longer "teach what they have always taught by teaching the way we've always taught." There can be little "down time" in a school anymore. Teaching time is precious and must be focused on ensuring that students learn. The principal must be out and about the school literally and figuratively as a way to monitor instruction.
- Principals will be called upon to be researchers. As students are tested for learning, the principal must work effectively with teachers to interpret student performance as research data and build strategies for intervention that will change that data for individual students and groups of data.
- More than ever, principals will need to spend quality time with parents to let them know about their students' progress and the progress of the school as a total organization. Parents must be seen as active partners in the education of their children and not simply as factors that need to be "dealt with" on occasion. Student progress (or lack of it) toward educational achievement

goals cannot be a surprise that parents hear at the end of the school year, after the grading period, or just after "the test scores come out."

- The principal must ensure that teachers understand their responsibilities to communicate with parents and students.

- As a principal, you will be called upon increasingly to be a public spokesperson for your school. Keep in mind one important tip: When questioned about disappointments in your school (e.g., test scores for the past year were lower than expected), it is critical that you explain but not provide excuses to the audiences that you face. Explanations suggest that improvement is possible or even likely because you know what happened. Excuses suggest that you and the school are hopeless and prone to accept "circumstances you cannot control."

- Above all, principals must appreciate that they are accountable in the performance of their assigned duties as leaders of student learning in their schools. They may no longer pass responsibility or blame to others if students or groups of students have problems.

In addition to these observations, what other changes do you see in your initial assumptions regarding your role as a principal in the age of professional responsibility and accountability in schools?

_____

_____

_____

_____

Adequate Yearly Progress

Another significant cornerstone in efforts to reform educational practice in states and across the nation may be found in the NCLB insistence that schools ensure that their students can be shown to be making reasonable progress toward achievement of important educational goals. This insistence is referred to frequently as the requirement for AYP by all students enrolled in all public schools.

According to the Education Commission of the States (2002), the following are critical issues to be addressed as a way to gauge whether AYP is being achieved in schools across the United States. Note that, in many cases, the exact definition of some criteria is left to individual states. You must become aware of the interpretations in your state.

1. AYP is measured primarily by gains in student achievement. However, individual states must make use of at least two additional indicators such as retention rates or high school graduation rates.

2. Each state must develop publicly known starting points or thresholds as a way to start the process of verifying student progress. These starting points were to be derived from achievement data collected during the 2001–02 school year.

3. Timelines must be developed to guide implementation. (NCLB requires all students in each state to be performing at or above proficient levels in reading and mathematics by the end of the 2013–14 school year.)

4. There should be continually increasing performance objectives over time, or annual minimum percentages of students and subgroups of students who are to meet or exceed proficiency in mathematics, reading, and language arts.

In the space below, describe the ways in which schools in your state are expected to achieve each of these mandated standards at present.

_____

_____

_____

_____

As an example of the ways in which individual states can "translate" the expectation of AYP into terms that are relevant to local needs, consider the following criteria of a school in the state of Texas for achieving AYP during the 2004–05 school year.

Texas schools, in order to meet AYP, must meet these criteria as a whole and in several socioeconomic and ethnic subgroups:

- A passing rate of at least 53% in reading and 42% on the TAKS (Texas Assessment of Knowledge and Skills) and other local assessments.
- A participation rate of at least 95% in any of the tests being used to measure performance.
- A graduation rate of 70% or higher.
- An attendance rate of 90% or higher. (Reeves, 2004)

Review your school's performance for the past two years and compare it to these indicators.

_____

_____

_____

_____

Ensuring Staff Quality

The terms of NCLB realize that no long-term improvement effort will ever take place without schools being staffed by teachers who are well-prepared and qualified to teach the subjects in which students are expected to attain certain achievement goals. NCLB defines "highly qualified teachers" as those who have obtained full state certification (including alternative teacher certification) or passed the state teacher licensing examination. All new elementary school teachers must hold at least a bachelor's degree and have passed a state test demonstrating content knowledge and teaching skills in reading, writing, mathematics, and other elementary curricular areas.

New middle and high school teachers are expected to hold at least a bachelor's degree and be able to demonstrate content area mastery in the subject they are teaching through success on a state licensing examination, as well as demonstrate successful completion of either graduate work, an undergraduate academic major, or advanced certification and credentialing.

Elementary, middle, or secondary school teachers not newly hired must hold at least a bachelor's degree and must also demonstrate academic content area knowledge. This demonstration may be subject to an exam but also must be based on multiple measures of teacher competency and be made available to the public upon request.

As you review the teachers who currently work in your school, to what extent are all of these individuals "highly qualified" in terms of NCLB?

_____

_____

_____

_____

In cases where teachers in your school may not currently meet the standards of being "highly qualified," what methods are available to assist these individuals in becoming formally qualified?

_____

_____

_____

_____

What strategies are in effect in your school or district to ensure that there is a high retention rate among those teachers who are highly qualified? (Put slightly differently, what are you doing to prevent good teachers from leaving your school, district, or the teaching profession in general?)

_____

_____

_____

_____

As you read over the expectations for highly qualified teachers, it may be interesting to note that required preservice learning includes only a bachelor's degree in an unspecified area (and in some cases, some additional graduate training, although not necessarily in educational fields). There is no demand that any teacher would have gone through a formal undergraduate teacher education program. There is clearly an assumption by politicians that teachers need only very strong content area backgrounds in order to be successful. No need is seen for specialized training in education in areas such as pedagogy, instructional design, student learning and development, classroom management, and many other issues that normally serve as the foundation for teacher training. What this may mean to you as a principal is that it may be possible, if not likely, that you will eventually have no teachers who have had formal training in such issues as lesson planning and development, testing, or many other areas viewed as traditional foundations for classroom teachers. To put it bluntly, there is a strong belief that "as long as you know the content, you can learn all the other stuff while on the job." Stated clearly, that means that your job as a principal will involve a good deal of teacher education and development work.

How many teachers who have gone through a nontraditional, alternative teacher certification program work in your school? What kinds of inservice programs will they need to follow in order to learn about teaching skills not covered during their undergraduate programs or in the alternative certification coursework?

_____

_____

_____

_____

What inservice education topics might be appropriate for all of your current teachers throughout this next school year?

_____

_____

_____

_____

Curriculum Reform

NCLB makes it clear that attention will need to be directed to curriculum refinement activities in each school. Based on results of standardized achievement testing during each year, school principals should be prepared to lead local efforts to modify and improve curriculum, particularly in the basic skill areas of reading, writing, and mathematics. In the case of elementary schools, particular attention needs to be directed toward the development of reading skills in primary grades. This is meant as a foundation for all student learning in all school curricular areas.

How do you assess your personal knowledge and skill in the area of reading instruction (whether you have an elementary, middle school, or high school background)?

_____

_____

_____

_____

If you are limited in knowledge and skill related to reading instruction, identify other individuals who work in your school and who will be helpful in your effort to promote stronger literary programs.

_____

_____

_____

_____

It is critical that all school principals across the nation continue to pay attention to the expectations found in NCLB. As noted earlier, whether you agree or disagree personally with the specific features of the legislation, a great percentage of the American public is convinced that this type of action is warranted to ensure that students in our public schools are learning and that taxpayers are getting a reasonable return for their investment of dollars. As an administrator, your job is often one of seeing that "the job gets done," not promoting philosophical discussions of relative worth and value.

THE REALITIES

Contrary to what Cyrus Castle shared with his beginning principal protégés in the opening scenario, the reality is that the expectation that schools will provide evidence to the public of their accomplishments is not a fad that will soon disappear. The belief that "this, too, shall pass" is not an idea that has much merit these days. Whether we like it or not, public schools in this country are viewed by critics as failed organizations. Even if you work in a school that is recognized repeatedly as an outstanding school where teachers, parents, and children are happy and achievement is clearly high according to all measures, you may be painted with the same broad brush to suggest that "our public schools are failing." The only way for any school to move forward despite such criticism is to continue to strive for the same excellent results as demonstrated in the past.

On the other hand, your first principalship may be in a school that does not have an exceptionally positive reputation. It may be a school where the former principal was moved involuntarily because achievement scores were low, absentee rates were high, and parent involvement was a rare feature. You have your work cut out for you to bring about change quite rapidly. If the parents of students at your school seem unconcerned about program quality, there will be other critics in the community who may actually enjoy finding your school to be an example of the "problems we have with public schools."

Reflecting again on what appeared to be the career of Cyrus Castle, the job of the principal has changed, and that is yet another reality that you face. Based on the information presented in the scenario, a "good principal" in Cyrus's day was a good golfer and a person who could "keep the lid" on the school, discipline students, mix well with important people in the community, and serve as a stern face in front of the school. Your job involves some of the named characteristics, but being a good golfer may not be as critical since you probably won't have enough time to play very much. Addressing issues associated with assuring parents and taxpayers that schools are producing students who are learning is not a fad. It will not "go away soon." Accountability is part of your job and it will remain a part of your job.

One last thing should be noted about the way your job as a principal will likely differ from past generations. More than ever, school principals have to be out in the community talking positively about their schools. We all have a great responsibility to assist the public to become committed to supporting and believing in the quality of their schools. Contrary to what many may think, American schools are doing great things for children. But we all have a duty to become cheerleaders for that fact as much as possible. If people believe in what you are doing, you will do greater things than you can now imagine.

YOUR PERSONAL PLAN

As noted in this chapter, much of your work as a principal will likely revolve around the expectations that are included in No Child Left Behind legislation. Specifically, this means that you will need to address expectations of greater accountability, such as expectations that your students will demonstrate adequate yearly progress. This, in turn, is determined in large measure through performance on standardized achievement testing.

What additional information do you believe you need to learn about measures of accountability in your state, your local district, and across the nation?

_____

_____

_____

_____

You are also responsible for ensuring that your teachers are highly qualified, at least in terms of knowledge of subject area content.

How do experienced principals in your school district address this expectation? How do you plan to ensure that your teachers are highly qualified?

_____

_____

_____

_____

Accountability expectations hold that, above all, students must be able to demonstrate learning in core curricular areas that include reading, writing, mathematics, science, and social studies.

How do you assess your personal ability to lead needed instructional and curricular development in these core areas?

_____

_____

_____

_____

REFERENCES

Business Roundtable. (2001). *Joint statement on the testing and accountability provisions of the Education Reform legislation.* Washington, DC: Author.

Education Commission of the States. (2002). Retrieved November 15, 2005, from http://www.ecs.org/

McLeod, D., D'Amico, J., & Protheroe, N. (2003). *The K–12 principal's guide to No Child Left Behind.* Reston and Alexandria, VA: National Association of Elementary School Principals and National Association of Secondary School Principals.

Reeves, D. B. (2004). *Accountability in action: A blueprint for learning organizations.* Englewood, CO: Advanced Learning Press.

Sunderman, G., Kim, J., & Orfield, G. (2005). *NCLB meets school realities: Voices from the field.* Thousand Oaks, CA: Corwin Press.

PART II

Socialization

Part II focuses on ways to feel more comfortable about your new role as a school principal. As noted earlier, newcomers often have a difficult time fitting in at a new school, district, and above all, profession. Among the most important lessons that are presented here are how to develop an awareness of what other people will expect of you and how to work toward becoming a part of your school and its community.

7

Seeing Your Invisible Heroes

Anna Ramirez had nearly 10 years of experience in several different administrative and supervisory roles in the district in which she had also spent a dozen years as a high school teacher. She worked in three different high schools in the school system. She had been an English and Language Arts coordinator working out of central office for three years; then she stepped in as a facilitator at the district's staff development center for two years. The past five years were spent as an assistant principal at Norman Rockwell High School for Fine Arts, an extremely well-respected magnet school that enrolled nearly 1,000 students. It not only provided a strong program in the study of art, but it also enjoyed a well-deserved reputation as a school with an extremely rigorous college prep curriculum. Anna was assistant principal for instruction, and she coordinated all instructional programs as well as curriculum and staff development in a school that had earned a statewide reputation for its challenging programs and placement of graduates into prestigious universities across the nation.

It was, therefore, somewhat surprising that during this past summer Anna applied for and received the principalship at Great Plains High School, an old building serving both a very wealthy community and several public housing projects. Great Plains had a fine reputation; many of its alumni had gone on to successful roles locally, nationally, and even internationally. It was not the nature of the school that seemed like a bad match for Anna, but rather that the school was truly a comprehensive high school with more than 3,000 students enrolled in programs ranging from basic remedial instruction to advanced placement courses. Anna's reputation as someone who worked very well with students in an advanced college prep school like Rockwell seemed inconsistent with her accepting a position at Great Plains. And people knew that Anna's expertise with curriculum and staff development would not be easily replaced at her former school. Still, Anna wanted the challenge of serving as a principal. She lived close to Great Plains and her own children graduated from the school. She knew that she would be working in a large school that faced significant challenges. But she knew that these challenges represented great opportunities, particularly for a "rookie" principal.

Anna's first few days in her office seemed to go smoother than she had anticipated. She felt very comfortable with her assignment. As teachers stopped in during the summer, she was pleased to note that many knew her already, either as a parent of former Great Plains students, or as a respected district staff development consultant, or as part of the leadership team at Rockwell. Anna had been concerned about her ability to relate effectively to a senior teaching staff. It was rare for a person with no previous experience as a principal to be sent to a school like Great Plains. But she had a strong background as a school leader, so she did not worry about the fact that she was stepping in as the new principal.

There were no problems during the summer before Anna's first school year as a principal. Contacts with teachers were fine, parents were very cooperative (perhaps because she knew many of them as neighbors as well), and she truly enjoyed her contacts with students. However, she started to realize that there were several people in the school who simply didn't seem to be very friendly to her. Among these were the secretaries, janitors, and the teacher aides who were now starting their new school year assignments. She decided that the best thing to do was to have a special meeting with these individuals before the school year started. In the past, she never had supervisory responsibility for her own noncertified and support staff, so she thought that it would be critical for these people to develop a strong understanding of what her expectations would be as soon as possible.

She arranged for the staff meeting to take place on the Friday afternoon before the first week of the school year. She very professionally described her background as an educator and listed the ways in which she believed that the staff could assist her in making certain that this year would be a success for every teacher, student, and parent. She reviewed the district policies regarding expectations for employees to report to duty each day on time, along with her requirements for reporting to her or designated assistant principals concerning the status of their work activity. She noted policies she expected to be followed in terms of sick leave, lunch time, use of telephones, and many of the kinds of things that she believed would allow the school to function more efficiently. Her goal was to let people begin to know her, her expectations, and the communication patterns she expected to be followed. Anna believed that the meeting went really well, although she was surprised that the group had no questions or comments about the issues she addressed. However, she realized that most of the staff had been at the high school for quite some time, so she assumed that their silence indicated that they had been well-trained and aware of their jobs in the school for many years. She considered herself to be quite fortunate to have such a loyal and happy group of employees.

On the following Monday, Anna was surprised to arrive at school at a bit after 7 a.m. and find three of the staff waiting on chairs just outside of her office. She greeted them, and Mary Fahey, the senior clerk in the front office, indicated that she and her two co-workers, Juan Mendez and Carla Wittmeyer, wanted to talk with her as soon as possible. Despite this being the day before students would arrive, Anna had quite a few "holes" in her schedule for the day, so she invited the trio into her office. Mary apparently was designated as the spokesperson for the group.

"Ms. Ramirez, the staff members met after your meeting with us last Friday afternoon, and they asked us to come to you to express a few things. First, we appreciate the fact that you have a very busy schedule, particularly since you are just taking over as the new principal. We understand that this is the first time you'll be in charge of a whole school, so we know there must be a lot of details you need to look into before tomorrow. But we are also here to share some concerns that our co-workers have after hearing your comments last week," Mary noted.

Anna was a bit surprised that there would be much of any kind of reaction from the workers. She really hadn't planned on any "fall-out" from what she thought had been a kind of cut-and-dried information session for the staff just before the school year began.

"Mary, I was only too happy to spend time with all of you last week. After more than 20 years in this business, I know how hard the cooks, janitors, and secretaries work each day. We couldn't live without the things you do for us. I really am a bit surprised that there were some concerns, however."

Mary looked at her two colleagues and was not really interested in responding immediately to the last comment by a person with whom she would be working closely this year. Juan Mendez, the head custodian at the high school, sensed Mary's hesitation, and so he jumped into the conversation.

"Ms. Ramirez, you know we want to do our jobs, but there's something that really bothered a lot of us. It may be a small thing, but just the titles you use are not quite right. For example, Mary is not even classified as a secretary. She is the senior clerk. The rest of us know her as a very important person who works here outside your door. She has been here for more than 20 years and has worked with five different principals during that time. She does a lot more than type and answer the phone. Carla is not just a cook. She runs the food services in this school. Because of her, we are able to feed nearly 3,000 students and almost 200 teachers and staff members every day. She and her colleagues plan menus, serve the meals, and Carla is responsible for a lot of money that comes from the federal government breakfast and lunch funds. And I and my team do a lot more than sweep floors and clean the bathrooms. We are responsible for the operation of a campus that takes up more than 60 acres of land. Every day, more than 3,000 adults and teenagers roam around a piece of land that is pretty big. We take care of the land and all of the people who use it here. So, if you don't mind, we would prefer to be called 'custodians' since we have been given the assignment to 'take custody' and care for everyone and the space that they occupy."

Anna was silent as she thought through the message she had been given. Her first inclination was to note the title changes and agree to that expectation. She would send the three of them back to report the findings of their work and everything would be fine for the clerks, custodians, and food service staff. But as she looked at the three who came to her, she began to realize that there was a lot more on their minds than simply getting new titles.

Carla was the next to speak. "The people here in the food service and other staff positions have been here a lot longer than almost all of the teachers. We have seen thousands of kids come and go. We go to football games because the players are 'our kids.' The same can be said about band performances, plays, academic contests, and many other events. The kids know us, and they know our names. Most teachers know us by name, but some still just look right through us every day when they see us in the halls. We feel as if we are invisible, but we often stay long after our duty times, even though we know the district cannot afford to pay overtime. Juan jump-starts teachers' cars on cold days; Mary hangs around until the last parent gets in to see you if they need your advice. And I have gone hungry a lot of days because we have had some sort of problem in the cafeteria just before lunchtime. We love this school and the students. But we need to know that the principal is aware of our concerns so that we feel like we are part of the team."

Suddenly, Anna felt a blend of pride that people like these folks were with her, but also guilt. Her comments last Friday made it seem like she was talking to a group of uncaring and unconcerned people who only work for a paycheck every two weeks. She suddenly realized that she was sitting with a group of educators, not people to be trained and monitored as if they did not really belong in the picture.

In your prior life as a classroom teacher, how many times did you work with a secretary or clerk?

_____

_____

_____

_____

When was the last time that you spent a minute or two talking with a custodian or food service worker, other than in terms of a "required conversation," such as "That parking lot looks like a mess. Can you get some brooms and clean up out there?" or "Don't forget that next Wednesday is 'Grandparents Day' and there will be quite a few guests joining their grandchildren for lunch"?

_____

_____

_____

_____

How many of the "invisible heroes" in your school do you know by name—first and last?

_____

_____

_____

_____

The literature on educational reform is filled with references to the fact that effective schools function as learning communities. In the literature related to business management, that term is changed slightly to "learning organizations." In education and the business world, this view is guided by the suggestion that organizations and schools will always be more successful and effective if they are operated based on a central theme, namely, that the more all members of the organization are included and involved with key decisions, the better things will be. In many ways, this is an expansion of an old phrase most of us learned as children: "Two heads are better than one." However, "two" now becomes "many" as a way to ensure that everyone with a stake in the success of an organization has a feeling of ownership in what takes place on a daily basis.

Traditionally, schools have operated according to a hierarchical framework, with administrative personnel on the top; professional (certified) teachers, counselors, and others at the next level below the top; and students at the bottom of the hierarchy. If you look at drawings that depict "typical" school organizations, you will also note that if noncertified (or classified) staff members are included at all in the diagrams, they are vaguely included along with the teachers. A review of the vast majority of textbooks about school administration ignore completely the role of support personnel, other than as a group that school administrators need to "deal with" as part of their work assignments each day. Simply stated, it is almost impossible for any school principal—beginner or veteran—to lead his or her school toward being a true "learning organization" or "learning community" if she or he relies on the traditional hierarchy at the school site level.

Creating "learning communities" or "learning organizations" is not a faddish term that has simply been coined in the last few years to encourage schools to create "touchy-feely" work environments. The business world has long recognized that when people who work in organizations feel they have an opportunity to influence what goes on in those organizations, there is a much greater likelihood of "buy-in" by all (Belasen, 2000). And that kind of investment leads inevitably toward greater productivity built on a sense that "this is our company" (Kofman & Senge, 1995). Roland Barth (1990), the founder of the Principals' Center at Harvard University, noted the great importance of building "buy-in" among all who work in schools:

> Central to my conception of a good school and a healthy workplace is community. In particular, I would want to return to work in a school that could be described as a community of learners, a place where students and adults alike are engaged as active learners in matters of special importance to them and where everyone is thereby encouraging everyone else's learning. (p. 9)

Peter Senge, author of the best-selling book *The Fifth Discipline* (1990), defined "learning organizations" in the following way:

> A learning organization is an organization in which people at all levels are, collectively, continually enhancing their capacity to create things they really want to create. (p. 20)

This chapter, then, is dedicated to the belief that everyone in a school should feel valued, listened to, and above all, respected because each person is a key contributor to the success of the school, which, in turn, is based on the success of students. A key group that you must work with, acknowledge, celebrate, and actually learn from are people I have referred to as the "invisible heroes" found in every school in this nation. These heroes include custodial staff, office workers, food service employees, paraprofessional and instructional aides, and everyone else who serves the needs of schools and students every day, but without being officially classified as part of the instructional staff. The list of specific job titles may include others such as security guards, bus drivers, and many other important jobs, but for the purposes of this chapter, I include only three broad groups of individuals, mostly because they are found in every school across the nation, regardless of size of school or district or grade level of students served. Virtually any school in which you may work has office workers, custodial staff, and food service workers.

OFFICE WORKERS

A piece of advice that has long been given to new principals is "treat your head clerk (or secretary) nicely because she or he knows all the secrets that are hidden in your school. Clerks are powerful people, so don't cross them." I agree with the basic sentiment in this statement but not with the suggested reason for paying attention to the people who work just outside your door. It is certainly true that they can create a great problem in a school by not doing their jobs correctly. And there is some truth in the notion that office staff have access to a great deal of information—both formal and informal—related to what happens in a school. But learning how to work with staff to ensure that you are not "double-crossed" in the future is not the major reason for respecting these people.

Perhaps the best way to think through the ways in which you might work effectively with secretaries and clerks is to reflect on some of the greatest "gripes" that these individuals have identified as bothersome. Among the issues most often identified as problems encountered by office staff are the following:

1. We are often treated as part of the office furniture rather than as real people.

It is often true that a new principal "inherits" most of the office staff in his or her new school. However, that observation does not mean that you need to think of the attendance clerk, the registrar, business manager, or the senior clerk or principal's secretary as pieces of furniture who will always be available to carry out tasks that you identify as important at a particular moment. Of course, you will know the name and background of your personal secretary rather quickly, but there are often many other individuals who work "just outside your door" who deserve personal recognition from the leader. An interesting observation in many schools is that teachers often know more about the secretarial staff than the principal does.

A suggestion is that you get to know the people you work with *as individuals* as quickly as possible upon coming into a new work environment. Begin by going through a kind of "crash course" to learn certain basic facts. In the space below, write down the names, job titles, and number of years of experience for each member of the office staff in your school.

_____

_____

_____

_____

Look at this list each time you go out to work stations in your building so that you get to know names, faces, and histories in this school (and other schools). It is amazing how quickly people respond positively to simply having another person *recall their name.*

2. Nobody really knows what we do here.

Again, this observation may not apply to the relationship between you and the person who acts as your immediate secretary or clerk. Within minutes of taking over as the new principal, you probably learned that the answer to "what my secretary does" is likely to include many different activities. But what about others who work in your main office? For example, what does an attendance clerk do? What pressures is she or he under regarding the reporting of absences and truancies each day? Have you ever stopped to take a look at the forms that must be completed accurately and in a timely fashion to ensure that your school is properly represented in districtwide reporting procedures?

Nobody expects that the principal would necessarily become an expert at each area of responsibility in a school. But taking the time to learn some of the basic skills that need to be addressed by office staff is a statement that you see individual contributions as a vital part of your school's success.

3. We are often treated as if we have no brains.

Often, office staff report that they believe that students (elementary or secondary) receive greater respect for their intellectual ability than do the members of the staff. Secretaries believe that they frequently are the last people to hear about new directions for schools. This is not simply a matter of individuals feeling "left out." It is critical to note that, in many cases, the first responders to rumors related to just about anything in the school are the people who first answer the phones. Thus, whether the issue that is being discussed centers on changes in the bell schedule, the adoption of a dress code for students, new curriculum, increased prices for cafeteria lunches, or just about anything else that may affect children, parents, or the community in general, it is important to keep people who interact directly with the community aware of what is going on. And when controversial matters are being considered by the administration and teachers, involve your staff with honest information about the issues under discussion. Remember the obvious that is often forgotten: Although your staff may not have college degrees or teacher certification, they are intelligent people who can have a tremendous impact on a community's sense of whether the school is open, honest, and effective.

Obviously, there are many other issues that serve to make office staff unhappy. Salaries are rarely commensurate with the responsibilities that people have in schools. Working conditions are often less than desirable; hot offices that often become filled with students facing disciplinary action, angry parents, and others are found in many schools. The expectations for individuals to carry out complex tasks without much training or support are frequent in school systems across the country. These may be issues faced by your office staff, but in most cases, they understand that the principal has very little control over such matters as salaries, fringe benefits, or even working conditions. But, like everyone else who comes in contact with your school, secretaries, clerks, and others who work in the office seek only one important type of recognition, and that is respect.

What are some additional ways in which you can develop effective professional relationships with the office staff of your school?

_____

_____

_____

_____

CUSTODIAL STAFF

Some have remarked that principals are often like mayors of small towns. They have great power and authority to carry out various required activities in their "towns." Their behavior and attitude are observed by all the "residents" as a constant indication of how things are going in the school. But mayors cannot do everything that is necessary to provide adequate services to all their citizens. That's why communities also hire people to work on street repairs and many other vital municipal services that ensure that safety, livability, and other indicators of a high quality of life are maintained.

The custodial staff of your school represents the team that makes your school safe and livable. For years, new and aspiring principals have been told that, in addition to the school secretary, the custodian is one of the two most critical people in your school. Like the school secretary, custodians can do a lot to make your daily life miserable if heating and cooling systems experience problems, plumbing is not fixed immediately, and classrooms are not cleaned adequately. These are worst-case scenarios. It is far better not to view your relationship with your custodial staff as a kind of insurance policy to prevent disaster. Instead, developing a mutual respect between you and those who are to maintain your school can have many very positive effects for everyone.

The most critical foundation for a positive relationship is the fact that you need to understand that a custodian is much more than "the guy who walks around the hallways with a broom or mop." To be sure, keeping a school clean is a central responsibility for a custodian. However, sweeping or mopping is not everything. As Juan Mendez said in the opening scenario, custodians are not only janitors. They have many more ways to contribute not only to school cleanliness, but overall well-being. Juan preferred to be called a custodian because he believed it represented the full range of his job responsibilities. The school was in "his custody" and care. Perhaps another term to use might be what our British colleagues use: school "caretakers." It is certainly not a bad idea to think about.

List some of the other things that your custodians do each day that go beyond their formal responsibilities such as cleaning, arranging meeting rooms, checking the heating and cooling system, inspecting the building for repairs and carrying out the repairs, and other similar activities traditionally associated with their jobs.

_____

_____

_____

_____

Custodians want the same consideration from their co-workers that was specified earlier by the office staff. For example, they want to be known by name and recognized as individuals, not just as workers around the building. It may be true that it is not easy to know all custodians individually. They often work in staggered shifts, where some custodians arrive very early in the morning before teachers and administrators report for work, or they work a shift that starts after the school day has concluded. In addition, there are often many custodians who work in a building. In a large high school, there may be as many as 20 different individuals who work in different corners of the campus. Consequently, it is not always easy to know each custodian as well as you know the office staff who tend to work in the same area each day. The key here is in the attitude that is demonstrated by you and the teachers when you encounter a staff member in the hall. Innovative practice, such as saying "Good morning" or asking "How are you today?" goes a long way to make people feel as if they belong.

Another thing custodians report that they value in schools is when people know that they really do much more than clean and pick up after people. We see men and women walking around with brooms and mops, and sometimes we forget that they do more than cleaning and maintenance work. It is up to each member of the school community to demonstrate respect for the myriad responsibilities and talents of every other member of the community. Remember, for example, that in addition to carrying a broom or wearing a tool belt around your school, your custodians also have lives out in the local community. They know people, and they are known and respected by others.

Like secretaries and other office staff members, custodians possess a great deal of knowledge about extremely important ways to assist you and others in operating your school more efficiently. As principal, you can assume that people had a great deal of confidence in your ability to provide leadership for the students in your school. You know a great deal about curriculum and instruction, staff evaluation, school site budgeting, and many other technical aspects of managing an educational organization. How to fix electrical or plumbing problems in a school may not be something in which you received special training. But having no electricity, or toilets that are broken, has a lot to do with whether your school operates effectively. Learn to rely on the expertise of others, from the counseling skills of people in your counseling office to the organizational skills of your office staff, to the practical knowledge of your custodial staff. You have a considerable amount of expertise around you; use it.

FOOD SERVICE WORKERS

"An army runs on its stomach!" So goes an old saying that describes the fact that when troops aren't fed, they don't fight very well. So officers need to do more than worry about battle tactics and strategies. They need to provide for basic human needs or the humans who work with them will not function very effectively.

Less than 100 years ago, schools did not include as part of their daily routines and duties the need to feed students and teachers. People either brought lunches from home, or they went home to have a lunch. Those days of cafeteria-less schools are gone. Today, American schools provide lunch and breakfast for millions of students each day. Food service is big business and a regular part of life in public schools.

As an administrator, you are aware that because operating funds are generally provided through resources of the federal government, food service programs function as separate enterprises within schools. They are not part of the "business" of running schools, other than that funding must be supervised at the local school district level. Therefore, the food service employees who work in your school are not, strictly speaking, part of your administrative concern. Your school has a designated food service manager who supervises employees and works toward providing students with free (or inexpensive) and nutritious meals each day.

Despite the nature of the relationship between the administration of your school and the operation of your school's food service program, the people who work in your cafeteria are important components of your school community. Virtually every student in your school will come in contact with the food service workers every day. It makes little difference that food service employees are often part-time workers because they work only during meal service times in your school. The fact is they deserve the same treatment as anyone else who serves the children in your school. The people who place food on cafeteria trays are educators in the sense that children observe their behavior and attitudes each day, and these can serve as powerful learning experiences whether they are officially noted as part of your school curriculum or not. It is critical that you, as the leader of your school community, do everything possible to demonstrate care and respect for the people "in the lunch line" who will have contact with the students. As is true of every person in your school, it is essential that you

- Demonstrate respect for the competence and contributions of each person
- Understand the unique abilities and skills of each person, regardless of his or her specific role
- Never forget that the ultimate goal of each encounter that you have with everyone has a potential positive effect on the lives and learning of your students

BUILDING A PERSONAL PLAN

The purpose of this chapter is to remind you that there are a lot of people who contribute to the effectiveness of a school. As a beginning principal, it is tempting to invest all of your time in addressing the needs of the primary actors in the school learning process, namely, students and teachers. It is easy to take others who are not directly in your line of sight for granted each day. In a good school, office staff, custodians, and food service workers go their own ways each day without much direct connection with the principal. But the fact is any school where community exists is a better place for students. To be a leader, you need to create the kind of culture and environment where community exists for all, even the people who work with you but who are often unseen or invisible.

To create a community where everyone is seen and involved, describe the people in your school who may not now be quite as visible to everyone, including yourself.

_____

_____

_____

_____

In what specific ways can you create an environment where everyone—students, teachers, administrators, and staff—can come together to share plans related to the creation of a community of trust, respect, and meaningful involvement of all?

_____

_____

_____

_____

In what ways do you believe it will be difficult to involve all members of your staff in the community?

_____

_____

_____

_____

How can you avoid these difficulties?

_____

_____

_____

_____

REFERENCES

Barth, R. S. (1990). *Improving schools from within.* San Francisco: Jossey-Bass.

Belasen, A. T. (2000). *Leading the learning organization.* Albany: SUNY Press.

Kofman, M., & Senge, P. (1995). Communities of commitment: The heart of the learning community. *Organizational Dynamics, 22*(2), 5–23.

Senge, P. (1990). *The fifth discipline: The art and practice of the learning organization.* New York: Doubleday.

SUGGESTED READING

Boyer, E. L. (1995). *The basic school: A community for learning.* Princeton: The Carnegie Foundation for the Advancement of Teaching.

Chawla, S., & Rednesch, J. (Eds.). (2001). *Learning organizations: Developing cultures for tomorrow's workplace.* Portland, OR: Productivity Press.

Marquardt, M. J. (1996). *Building the learning organization.* New York: McGraw Hill.

Speck, M. (1999). *The principalship: Building a learning community.* Upper Saddle River, NJ: Prentice Hall.

8

Parents as Partners?

Bobbi Clements felt really good about her school, Chamberlain Heights Primary. She had taken over the principalship in January, shortly after the former principal, Dr. Carl Everett, announced that he was going to retire due to a medical condition that would make it quite difficult to carry out the duties associated with effective school leadership. Dr. Everett was a local hero, having served the Chamberlain Heights community for nearly 30 years. Bobbi knew that following such an individual into her first principalship would not be an easy task. While she had some personal disagreements with some of Dr. Everett's policies and practices, she knew that she had to be discreet in cases where she wanted to follow a new path. Serving as an assistant principal for four years in a middle school taught her many important skills and gave her many valuable insights. One of these was the importance of being careful if you follow a "legend." This would be a great challenge but one well worth it because Chamberlain Heights was a great school with outstanding teachers.

One of the things that Bobbi disagreed with her predecessor about was the ways in which he worked with parents in his community. She was told that he had little patience for "whining" or "threatening" by mothers and fathers. He also defined effective school-community relations as two parents' nights per year and occasional visits by parents who were concerned about some aspect of their child's academic progress. Like all schools in the state, Chamberlain was required to have parents sit as regular members of the Campus School Improvement Committee (CSIC). Dr. Everett simply appointed two teachers who happened to have children attending the school, and they served as the parent members of the committee.

Although there was every indication that Dr. Everett was well-respected as the "heart of Chamberlain Heights" for many years, it was not entirely surprising that within the first two weeks of Bobbi's term as the new principal she had been visited by several local parents who wanted to express an interest in becoming more involved with the school. The new principal decided that this was one area where changes from the past administrative style were necessary. She announced her desire to make Chamberlain a more "parent friendly school" at the next faculty and staff meeting.

Bobbi had expected that the majority of her colleagues would be quite pleased to hear of her interest in making the school more accessible to parents and other members of the community. She was surprised, however, that when she indicated that the CSIC would now be open to parents in the community who did not necessarily have any ties to the faculty, she faced a sea of unfriendly faces in the audience.

"But Ms. Clements, you don't understand the parents around here. If you start to involve them with one activity, they'll be all over this school trying to run everything. Dr. Everett worked hard to keep them out of our hair so we could do our jobs as teachers," said Mrs. Tilly Winkle, a kindergarten teacher who was the only teacher in the school who had been there before Dr. Everett had arrived.

Willie Harris, a first-grade teacher with three years of experience, was next to voice his concerns. "I don't mind having parents drop in for conferences any time they need, and I surely don't mind having parents coming in as volunteers. But it's like Dr. Everett said, 'You have to control them before they try to control us.'"

Bobbi was astounded at the reaction for two reasons. First, it was clear that Carl Everett's spirit was still wandering the halls of "his" school. She had expected that, to some extent. In light of the obvious affection that so many still had for him, Bobbi knew that she would have to approach that issue very carefully. Only time would cause the memories to fade, and she didn't want to start a war over what was really only a minor matter in her mind.

More significant was the apparent view that the school belonged to the teachers and staff and that parents were nuisances that had to be endured. The only really positive thing that she heard was Mr. Harris's acceptance that parent volunteers could be an asset at times. This issue was one that Bobbi could not afford to put on the back burner. She didn't enjoy the clout in the community that would keep parents away. Besides, she didn't want to keep the walls up. She really believed in the decal that was found on the front door of her school: "To all parents and visitors, welcome to Chamberlain Heights Primary School. This is your school. We appreciate your involvement."

Most schools have decals or signs in front to signify the sentiments that Bobbi saw on the door of Chamberlain Heights. It is always a bit questionable whether these statements are sincere indications to parents that they are truly welcome. These days, there is understandable caution regarding nonschool personnel being able to walk around a school without any challenge. However, the sentiments expressed by Bobbi Clements's teachers are not unusual. Simply stated, the attitude in many schools is "we will allow parents in here, but only on our terms."

There are many clear indications that it is no longer acceptable for schools to exclude parental involvement. The expectation in most states now is that parents will be involved regularly in the decision-making process of local schools through participation in such bodies as the CSIC in the opening scenario. Site-based decision making is no longer an experiment tried in a few districts. Whether it is correct or not, states are now proclaiming that parents must be viewed as partners in the education of their children. This is further underscored by the fact that, as I noted in Chapter 6, it is now possible nationally (through the terms of No Child Left Behind legislation) for parents to remove their children from schools that do not demonstrate adequate yearly progress for three years in a row. Of course, there are critics who note that these additional opportunities for parental control of education are not accompanied by equivalent demands for parents to become actively involved in their children's education through oversight of homework, making certain that children are on time, or even ensuring that students attend school at all. In fact, schools (and school principals) are now held accountable for ensuring that parents have opportunities for regular involvement in their local schools.

As a result of these factors, it is no longer simply a desirable practice for principals to work toward effective relations with parents. It is now an expectation to ensure participation. In addition to all of the other matters we have considered as part of your duties as a beginning principal, you must also devote time and energy to "look outward" from your school and find ways to ensure parents feel a part of their children's education.

TRADITIONAL FUNCTIONS OF HOME-SCHOOL RELATIONS

Effective home-school relations are the result of a systematic and concentrated effort by the school to address three aims. First, opportunities can be increased for parents and other citizens to work, as appropriate, with school administrators, teachers, and others to make meaningful decisions affecting the school. Second, efforts may be directed toward ensuring that effective multidirectional communication occurs among the home, the school, and the community. Third, the school is able to devise ways to utilize community resources to enhance its educational program.

Involvement in Decision Making

School practices are improved when people who have an interest in the outcome of a decision have a chance to participate in its making. Many schools do a good job of involving people within their walls in decision making. Administrators, teachers, staff members, counselors, and students frequently participate in decision making by serving on task forces, councils, or committees. If such opportunities exist for people in the school, parents and other community members should have a way to become involved as well. The assumption is that many different groups have much to contribute to the quality of decisions.

There is a research base that suggests strongly that parental involvement in schoolwide decision making has a direct positive impact on the quality of education in an individual school. Noel Watkins (1978) studied parental involvement in high schools and noted the following:

1. The presence of parents on schoolwide decision-making groups and committees adds needed parental and community perspectives to many different issues.

2. Continuous interaction with parents causes educators to be more client-centered in their thinking.

3. Participation by parents and other community members helps school staffs legitimize decisions in the eyes of the community. (pp. 37–38)

The fact that there are demonstrable positive effects derived from the involvement of parents in school decision making is likely to be the reason so many districts and states now require the creation of schoolwide decision-making groups for each school. The state of Texas (and other states) requires that each school organize and meet regularly with campus-based educational improvement committees throughout each school year. The Chicago Public Schools, as part of a massive reform initiative in the early 1990s, created Local School Committees to guide the work of each of the nearly 1,000 schools in the district. In both cases, the inclusion of parents has always been seen as the central ingredient in any local educational improvement efforts.

In your experience, what is the additional value of including parents as regular members of groups designed to address schoolwide issues?

_____

_____

_____

_____

A concern, of course, in encouraging broad-based community participation in school decision making is that many meetings deal with issues that have little immediate interest to people outside of the school. When the agendas of meetings are filled with daily school operational concerns, parents can become quickly disenchanted.

Are there other limitations that you see to the involvement of parents and other community members in the decision-making processes of an individual school?

_____

_____

_____

_____

Another way to involve parents is through ad hoc participation. In this way, people can become involved only in issues of particular interest. An example of such an arrangement would be the establishment of a task force composed of teachers, students, parents, staff members, and administrators for the purpose of developing a dress code policy for the school.

What are some ways in which you have seen parents involved in ad hoc task forces or committees? How effective have these been in increasing school quality?

_____

_____

_____

_____

A third way to promote greater parental involvement is for the school to establish permanent special advisory groups to enable community representatives to have a continuing role in making recommendations regarding specific concerns. Such groups have long been associated with activities in high schools. Consider, for example, booster groups for sports teams and marching bands. This same notion might be expanded for other grade levels and other activities in local schools.

Have you had experience working with specialized advisory groups of parents? What were the advantages of these groups existing in a school?

_____

_____

_____

_____

Fostering Effective Two-Way Communication

Traditionally, communication between the school and its community has been confined to newsletters, bulletins, and periodic announcements through the media (Fruth, Bowles, & Moser, 1977; Whitaker & Fiore, 2001). Although such modes of communication are useful, they represent only a small part of what is needed to establish and foster effective communication between the home and the school. Perhaps the greatest problem with typical communication channels is that they are one-way devices—the school tells only its side of the story (Daresh, 1986).

Lines of communication from the community to the school must be opened as well. Traditional two-way communication devices include open houses, "back to school" nights, parent-teacher association meetings, and parent conferences. These are all helpful, but they often do little to assist parents and other community members interested in coming together on a continuing basis to share mutual concerns about educational processes.

What strategies designed to increase stronger lines of communication from the school to the home (and reverse) have you seen that might be useful?

_____

_____

_____

_____

Home-school-community relations and their aim of fostering more effective communication must be an integral part of the philosophy and standard procedures of the school, not a haphazard arrangement where parents and other community members are occasionally invited into the school.

Utilizing Community Resources

The third aim of an effective home-school-community relations program is to utilize the resources found in a community as a way to enrich the quality of a school's total educational program. Schools are no longer able to be the sole providers of all the requisite skills and knowledge that students need to thrive in society. The expertise of many people must be tapped and made available so that each student may be prepared to deal with complex future demands.

There are two basic approaches to making the community an educational resource. In some cases, community representatives are occasionally drawn into the school as resource persons. This approach might include having guest speakers for individual classes, and also using community representatives in an advisory capacity for some instructional programs.

Indicate your experiences with inviting local community representatives to serve as resources to enrich your school's educational program.

_____

_____

_____

_____

Another approach to using community resources is to send students out into the community for experiential learning programs. Going out into the community for field trips and other experiences has long been recognized as a valuable activity. Even more ways of utilizing the community as a learning site may be found in the future.

Provide some examples of how your students might be able to enhance their own learning through experiences in the community.

_____

_____

_____

_____

CURRENT PROBLEMS WITH SCHOOL-COMMUNITY RELATIONS

The ideal situation that should be appealing to any school is the creation of true partnerships with parents so that all three of the aims of effective home-school-community relations noted above could be attained. It would be great if parents and others could be involved in making meaningful decisions to improve the school, engage in ongoing positive two-way communication, and find opportunities for learning out in the community. In fact, that ideal is rarely achieved in a great majority of schools. However, as a beginning principal, your goal may be to move your school toward a better relationship with the world outside your door. Remember, too, that the perceptions of parents will always have a great impact on the ways in which many others see your efforts to serve as a strong instructional leader.

Relations between teachers (and others who work in schools) and parents continue to be problematic, as evidenced by the different perceptions of these two important groups.

Teacher Perceptions of Parents

Most teachers would probably prefer to have positive interactions with parents. As most people who work around schools know, however, developing and maintaining such relations are often difficult. And many of the problems that lead to this situation come from the perceptions that teachers and other educators have regarding parents. Some of these views are noted below.

• Parents are unaware of any student needs other than the immediate needs of their own children.

While it is certainly understandable that parents would develop some tunnel vision regarding the needs of their own children, they must realize that schools are social organizations where the needs of many students must be addressed in an equitable fashion. The important stance that the principal must take regarding this issue is to walk a line of reassurance so that teachers as well as parents understand that working for all does not necessarily mean forgetting about any. In other words, if there are small groups of students with special needs (e.g., developing better reading skills), the teacher will not ignore this minority of learners while proceeding with the instruction of the majority.

How can teachers address individual student needs without ignoring all the others in their classes? (Remember, parents are usually reasonable people who can appreciate the difficulties of focusing on one and all at the same time, so they do not necessarily expect miracles. All most parents want is sincere attention to their children.)

_____

_____

_____

_____

• Parents have inflated notions of the abilities and talents of their own children.

Again, this is understandable. If you have ever been an athletic coach, theater director, or school newspaper sponsor, you know that every student comes to your program as the star of the team, outstanding thespian, and gifted writer. In all cases, they deserve better parts, more playing time, and bigger bylines. Teachers sense the same behaviors on the part of many parents who believe that their children should get no lower than an "A" or always get perfect scores on every homework assignment or exam. In the minds of some teachers, this type of attitude makes parents difficult to work with.

What approaches might you take with parents who seek "star status" for their children, or for teachers who feel that parents demonstrate expectations for their children that are not realistic?

_____

_____

_____

_____

- Parents will sue you at the drop of a lawyer's business card.

It is true that American society is increasingly swayed toward legal action as a remedy for any real or imagined problem. It is even likely that parents of children in your school will exercise their ability to take legal action against you, your teachers, staff members, the superintendent, the school board, and anyone who gets in the way of their interest to protect their children. Teachers are increasingly aware that parents of many students (particularly those with special needs) are more assertive with regard to seeking support for their children. And schools and teachers have indeed been found guilty of a variety of actions that border on misfeasance and even malfeasance. But not every parent is planning to file suit against every teacher, although there is often a perception among teachers that "one false step and you'll be in court." The net effect of such attitudes is that they may have a devastating impact on the ability to promote open communication between your school and many parents.

In what ways can you work with teachers to alleviate their fears regarding the possibility of unpleasant legal actions being brought by discontented parents?

_____

_____

_____

_____

How can you, as the principal, work directly with parents to reduce levels of tension and conflict when these factors begin to emerge and threaten the teachers and staff of your school?

_____

_____

_____

_____

- There is no real reason to waste time trying to get parents involved with schools. They really do not want to be there in the first place.

There is a great deal of truth in the observation that parental involvement decreases as their children proceed through school. It's not difficult to get great turnouts of parents for primary school children, but by the time children go to middle schools or high schools, parent attendance at school events falls off significantly. Why bother to even get interested in parental involvement that won't happen because parents just don't care?

How can you work effectively with teachers to plan and carry out events that will appeal to parents who may not feel as if their attendance at school events is actually valued by teachers and administrators?

_____

_____

_____

_____

In addition to the issues noted here, what other views do teachers express concerning problems that they experience with efforts to work effectively with parents?

_____

_____

_____

_____

Parent Concerns

Problems with the establishment of effective relationships between the school and parents are also based on concerns held by parents. Former Chicago area principal Elaine McEwan (2005) presents a comprehensive and very helpful analysis of parent behaviors and concerns that cause an undesirable gulf between parents and schools. She notes that modern parents

- are less respectful of authority (not just in school settings, but in many other public settings);
- are more educated about education (and feeling more empowered to assert their views because of such movements as NCLB and special education legislation);
- are angrier than ever (and they are more likely to be reluctant to express anger and frustration with educators);
- are increasingly cynical and distrustful (and unwilling to trust in many societal institutions such as schools, churches, and so forth);
- have commitment to serve as social activists (and therefore more inclined to seek flaws and problems in schools so that social action can be promoted to cure what is wrong);
- are stressed resulting from complicated personal and professional lives;
- are worried and fearful because they are sincerely not certain that their children will succeed in future years after going through schools which they hear so frequently are not equal to the task of preparing students for future challenges.

While many specific causes might be cited for these general factors, McEwan (2005) notes the following issues that are related to the interactions that occur regularly between parents and the educational community, and which drive many of the current problems in the area of effective school-community relations:

- The world in which we live is filled with influences and circumstances that often foster hostility, rage, and out-of-control behavior.
- Educators often unwittingly or even intentionally upset parents with the things they do and say.
- Education is characterized by broad swings of philosophy and methodology, a steady stream of innovations that often defy logic, and constant pleas to the public for more money to solve its problems, creating the belief among some that educators don't know what they're doing.

- Parents have pervasive family dynamics or personal psychological, emotional, and behavioral problems that impact the ways in which they interact with almost everyone, but most especially educators. (p. 7)

The by-product of these issues is increasingly a situation in which parents of school-age children demonstrate the kinds of attitudes and beliefs that contribute to the issues faced by teachers.

I would add another significant cause for many of the educational problems that now face parents and add to the malaise gripping communication between the interests of the public and the interests of public education. Many recent reform efforts have unwittingly had the effect of pulling the two worlds further apart. Consider, for example, the terms of NCLB, which offer a blueprint for parents to remove their children from school based solely on the outcomes of achievement testing that, admittedly, serves as only one indicator of a school's overall worth and effectiveness. The message is quite clearly stated that schools are under a threat of severe sanction and perhaps even closure if test scores are low. The implication of this is that parents wield considerable power, yet little is suggested in terms of the concomitant responsibilities that parents have to join with local schools in creating more effective learning for children. In short, while public schools are expected to respond to mandates for greater accountability, public school parents are rarely, if ever, expected to demonstrate the same adherence to a model where people are held accountable for individual actions.

These issues contribute to an ever-widening division between the world of teachers and the world of parents. You are in the middle as the principal. While you wish to support your teachers, you are also aware that good working relationships with parents are important as well. But you cannot afford to support every action by every teacher every time because teachers do make mistakes that need to be addressed. And taking the side of parents in all cases results in principal behavior exemplified by things such as constant movements of children from one teacher's class to another simply because "my child doesn't like the teacher," or forcing coaches and other teachers to add players to the baseball team (or soccer team, or the band, the newspaper staff, and so forth) to appease demanding parents who are angry or frustrated because they want good things to happen to their children (and in some cases, want you to endorse their parenting skills). Remember that the actions you take in the first few years of your principalship will follow you well into the future. Angering parents now will cast you as a principal who "cannot work well with the community." Always taking the side of parents will signal that you do not support teachers.

So the responsibility, ultimately, is one that falls squarely on your shoulders to make some value judgments now, as a relatively inexperienced principal and administrator. Always think clearly what the outcomes of any decision will be in terms of relationships between parents and teachers. This is a matter of being acutely aware of the planks in your personal educational platform. As I reviewed the process of developing this personal statement in an earlier chapter, it was made clear that whenever a person articulates a personal belief, consequences will follow. As was true of Bobbi Clements in the opening scenario, it is critical to give direction as a leader by taking a stand quickly, though quietly. No speeches were needed by the new principal to decry the legendary Carl Everett's efforts to eschew parental involvement at Chamberlain Heights. But a change in direction was needed.

How would you describe your attitude regarding the proper ways in which parents can effectively be involved in schools?

_____

_____

_____

_____

Considering your current school and staff, what positive and negative consequences would working with parents have for your ability to lead effectively as the new principal? What would the consequences (positive and negative) be for the school and the quality of learning for students?

Positive: _____

_____

_____

_____

_____

Negative: _____

_____

_____

_____

YOUR PERSONAL PLAN

An absolutely nonnegotiable part of the job of being a school principal involves the ability to work effectively and productively with parents and others in your community. How you choose to take on that duty may be greatly affected by your personal values, beliefs, and platform. How far you are willing to go to implement an effective program of school-community relations is also a plank in your platform. But you must do it, as surely as you must maintain a safe and secure building, oversee instruction through regular evaluation of teachers, and carry out many other responsibilities of being a principal.

But simply stating that you are responsible for an effective program of school-community relations does not mean that such activity can easily be carried out by you alone. Perhaps more than any other leadership responsibility, communicating effectively with parents is something that requires the participation of the entire school community of teachers and staff. You can announce that you look forward to working with parents, but if teachers are rude to visiting mothers and fathers, if telephone calls are not returned, and if teachers do not enthusiastically participate in parent conference sessions, your words will be hollow, indeed. As a result, your personal plan in this important area must go beyond simply stating what you believe or what you should do. Here, you need to identify strategies that might involve convincing others or attempting to change others' behaviors and attitudes.

How will you assess the perspectives of all your teachers and staff members regarding their preferred levels of involvement by parents in the school?

_____

_____

_____

_____

After your discussions with staff members, what would you say are the most positive aspects of the school culture related to communication with parents and other community members?

_____

_____

_____

_____

Where are the areas of resistance toward contact and effective working relationships with parents?

_____

_____

_____

_____

What are some strategies that you plan to follow to build upon the positive aspects of your school's culture as a way to influence some of the negative features you have identified?

_____

_____

_____

_____

In three years, where do you hope to see your school with regard to effective communication with parents and other community members?

_____

_____

_____

_____

REFERENCES

Daresh, J. C. (1986, March). Effective home-school-community relations for secondary school improvement. *The Clearing House, 59*(7), 312–315.

Fruth, M., Bowles, B. D., & Moser, R H. (1977). Home-school-community relations in IGE. In H. J. Klausmeier, R. A. Rossmiller, & M. Saily (Eds.), *Individually guided education: Concepts and practices* (pp. 216–237). New York: Academic Press.

McEwan, E. K. (2005). *How to deal with parents who are angry, troubled, afraid, or just plain crazy* (2nd ed.). Thousand Oaks, CA: Corwin Press.

Watkins, A. N. (1978). *Decision making processes in senior high schools that individualize instruction.* Madison, WI: Wisconsin Research and Development Center for Individualized Schooling.

Whitaker, T., & Fiore, D. J. (2001). *Dealing with difficult parents and with parents in difficult situations.* Larchmont, NY: Eye on Education.

9

Others' Expectations

When Frank Lujan accepted his current position as the principal of Graystone Elementary School, he felt a mixture of both confidence and anxiety to an extent that he had never quite felt before in his professional life. He believed that he had enough experience as a teacher to appreciate some of the major issues that needed to be addressed in an effective elementary school. He had also learned enough in the traditional areas of law, finance, supervision, and personnel management when he completed his graduate degree at State University two years ago.

On the other hand, Frank was not totally comfortable with the expectation that others had for his performance. He knew that he wanted to spend a lot of time working with teachers to help them improve their efforts in helping the kids. That seemed to be a statement that made a lot of sense to those who talked with him during the three interviews that preceded his getting this job. However, last week, when the superintendent met with all the new principals in the district, Frank heard a somewhat different message about getting the year off to a good start by taking charge of things through sharing personal visions and goals with the teachers and staff. Back at State University, Frank's mentor and advisor, Dr. Norma Galloway, always told him that his most critical job as a beginning principal was to make certain that "the chalk was in the classrooms and the light bulbs were illuminating the hallways and the thinking around the school." That was Dr. Galloway's approach to letting Frank know that she believed the technical and managerial details of the principal's job were very important.

Frank was truly looking forward to his new life as a school principal, but in fact, he was more than a bit confused about whose voice he should be hearing now that the school year was about to get under way.

Frank Lujan is certainly not the only beginning principal who has been given so much good advice that he has not been given any advice at all. In fact, just about everyone will have a different idea about what you should be doing now that you are in charge. In the long run, you will have to make your own decisions about what should be done, by whom, and how you should define your job as a principal. But it is critical to note that there are likely to be numerous competing discussions and descriptions of that job.

This chapter tackles the issue of these competing expectations. Research findings are presented about what different individuals such as superintendents, experienced principals, and aspiring principals have to say about the most important aspects of your job. In the long run, you will have to be the person who decides what is most critical about your work, but some alternative perspectives that may be of interest to you are also shared.

CRITICAL SKILLS FOR BEGINNING PRINCIPALS: A SURVEY

Before going any further with this discussion of the kinds of skills that different groups expect of you as a beginning principal, you may wish to take a moment to respond to the items on the survey in Table 9.1, the Beginning Principal's Critical Skills Inventory. This instrument was developed a few years ago to do the research that serves as the basis for this chapter.

Scale 1 (Items 1–8) deals with the items that are associated with the technical and managerial duties of school principals. These tend to be the kinds of responsibilities that are found in job descriptions or policy manuals of many school districts. Scale 2 (Items 9–16) deals with issues that are defined as socialization skills, or things that a person needs to know, do, or demonstrate to fit comfortably into a new organization. Finally, Scale 3 (Items 17–24) is composed of items that are self-awareness skills, or items that touch on one's personal ability to know one's values, attitudes, beliefs, and dispositions as they are related to the professional role of an educational leader.

Now that you've had a chance to complete the Beginning Principal's Critical Skills Inventory, you have rank-ordered the three broad categories of technical and managerial skills (Scale 1), socialization skills (Scale 2), and self-awareness skills (Scale 3). The next section of this chapter looks at your ratings as they compare with those of other individuals who also participated in this research over the past few years. You should soon appreciate the fact that even among professional school administrators with many years of experience, there is little consensus as to the "ideal" duties of principals.

Other Beginners

You were in line with the majority of other beginners (i.e., principals in their first, second, or third year on the job) who also participated in this research if you rank-ordered the three skill areas from most to least important as follows:

1. Technical Skills

2. Socialization Skills

3. Self-Awareness Skills

Table 9.1   Beginning Principal's Critical Skills Inventory

Directions: For each of the following duties assigned to principals, please assess the extent to which each item is critical to your ability to do your job. Use the following scale in responding to each item:

5 = Extremely important

4 = Somewhat important

3 = Neutral (not extremely important or totally unimportant)

2 = Somewhat unimportant

1 = Totally unimportant

Scale (Circle one)   **Item** _____

5 4 3 2 1   1. Knowing how to evaluate staff (i.e., procedures for the task and also the substance: What do standards really mean?).

5 4 3 2 1   2. Knowing how to facilitate/conduct group meetings.

5 4 3 2 1   3. Knowing how to design and implement a data-based improvement process, including goal setting and evaluation.

5 4 3 2 1   4. Knowing how to develop and monitor a school-based budget.

5 4 3 2 1   5. Knowing how to organize and conduct parent-teacher-student conferences.

5 4 3 2 1   6. Knowing how to establish a scheduling program (master schedule) for students and staff.

5 4 3 2 1   7. Awareness of issues related to school staff.

5 4 3 2 1   8. Knowing how to manage food service, custodial, and clerical staff.

5 4 3 2 1   9. Establishing a positive and cooperative relationship with other district administrators.

5 4 3 2 1   10. Knowing how to determine who is what in a school setting.

5 4 3 2 1   11. Knowing how to relate to school board members and central office personnel.

5 4 3 2 1   12. Knowing where the limits exist with the district or building and balancing that knowledge with one's own professional values.

5 4 3 2 1   13. Understanding how the principalship changes family and other personal relationships.

5 4 3 2 1   14. Developing interpersonal networking skills that may be used with individuals inside and outside the system.

5 4 3 2 1   15. Ability to encourage involvement by all parties in the educational system.

5 4 3 2 1   16. Knowing how to develop positive relationships with other organizations and agencies in the school's surrounding community.

5 4 3 2 1   17. Demonstrating an awareness of what it means to possess organizational power and authority.

(Continued)

Table 9.1 (Continued)

5	4	3	2	1	18. Demonstrating an awareness of why one was selected for the leadership position in the first place.
5	4	3	2	1	19. Portraying a sense of self-confidence on the job.
5	4	3	2	1	20. Having a vision along with the understanding needed to achieve organizational goals.
5	4	3	2	1	21. Demonstrating a desire to make a significant difference in the lives of students.
5	4	3	2	1	22. Being aware of one's biases, strengths, and weaknesses.
5	4	3	2	1	23. Understanding and seeing that change is ongoing and that it results in a continually changing vision of the principalship.
5	4	3	2	1	24. Knowing how to assess job responsibilities in terms of the real world role of the principal.

Scoring: Now add up your scores in the following ways

    Scale 1:   Items 1—8   = _____ divided by 8 = _____

    Scale 2:   Items 9—16 = _____ divided by 8 = _____

    Scale 3:   Items 17—24 = _____ divided by 8 = _____

Rank order your three average scores per scale:

        _____

        _____

        _____

In addition, you were consistent with a high percentage of aspiring principals (people currently enrolled in university preparation programs leading to state certification or licensure).

Of all 24 items on the survey, which one did you believe to be the single most important item? Why?

_____

_____

_____

_____

Which was the least important item? Why?

_____

_____

_____

_____

Research has found that beginning principals and people who were enrolled in training programs leading to certification as principals most frequently chose Item 7, "Awareness of issues related to local school law," as the most critical to be demonstrated by principals, whereas Item 18, "Demonstrating an awareness of what it means to possess organizational power and authority," was viewed as the least important skill.

What do you think these responses imply in terms of the perceptions held by colleagues who are not yet in the principalship or who have recently stepped into their first administrative assignment?

_____

_____

_____

_____

Experienced Principals

Of the 24 items on the Beginning Principal's Critical Skills Inventory, which did you believe were rated as most important by principals with at least three years of experience? Why?

_____

_____

_____

_____

Which items from the survey were probably listed as least important by the experienced principals? Why?

_____

_____

_____

_____

According to the principals who responded to this research, the most critical skill to be demonstrated by a beginning principal was Item 10, "Knowing how to determine who is what in a school setting." This item was followed closely by Item 9, "Establishing a positive cooperative relationship with other district administrators." Both of these were in the cluster of items related to socialization skills.

According to practicing principals, the items least relevant for successful beginning colleagues were Item 8, "Knowing how to manage food service, custodial, and secretarial staff," and Item 6, "Knowing how to establish a scheduling program (master schedule) for students and staff." These items, and most others that were among the lowest-ranked issues, were clustered in the technical and managerial skills category.

What do you believe are some of the reasons why experienced principals appear to value socialization skills demonstrated by newly appointed colleagues while they seem to emphasize less the skills in the managerial and technical domain?

_____

_____

_____

_____

Superintendents

The last group of educators that responded to this survey were superintendents who had hired new principals in their school districts during the last three years. Their reasons followed very different patterns from those of beginning and experienced principals. What items do you believe that superintendents viewed as the most critical for beginning principals? Why do you believe these skills were viewed as so important?

_____

_____

_____

_____

Table 9.2   Skills Priority Comparison for School Administrators

	Beginning Principals'	Experienced Principals'	Superintendents' Ranking
Technical/Managerial Skills	1	3	3
Socialization Skills	2	1	2
Self-Awareness Skills	3	2	1

What do superintendents view as the least important skills for the beginning school administrator? Why?

_____

_____

_____

_____

Of all the skills listed in the Beginning Principal's Critical Skills Inventory, the one indicated as most important by superintendents with recent experience selecting at least one principal for their district, and also with experience working with these new principals, was Item 18, "Demonstrating an awareness of why one was selected for a leadership position in the first place." Second on the list of priorities valued by superintendents was Item 19, "Portraying a sense of self-confidence on the job."

The lowest items on the superintendents' lists were Item 8, "Knowing how to manage food service, custodial, and secretarial staff," and Item 6, "Knowing how to establish a scheduling program (master schedule) for students and staff."

In terms of the broad categories of skills measured by the survey, Table 9.2 shows how the priorities of the three groups surveyed look when compared.

SO WHAT DOES THIS MEAN?

The fact that three different groups hold different expectations for what principals are supposed to do is not a new or astonishing finding. However, the study reported here has provided some important insights into differences that, in turn, are related to finding more ways to guide people through personal career transitions and also provide people with more effective experiences as beginning school principals.

The implications of this research are clear concerning induction programs designed to assist novice school administrators. For example, the findings of this study suggest that experienced principals and superintendents value colleagues' abilities to fit into the social context of the school district. This offers a great argument in favor of adopting mentoring schemes for new principals. Chapter 14 will review this topic in greater detail. Here, it should be noted that mentoring for new principals is often missing the mark about the real issues facing beginners. The majority of existing mentoring programs tend to focus on helping people learn critical technical and managerial skills associated with work in a particular school system. Since the funding for mentoring is most often provided by local school systems, it makes sense that the primary focus of support would be on the immediate needs of the district: how to do the district paperwork, how to implement local policies, dealing with priorities and politics in the immediate community, and so forth. However, it may be considerably more important for a district to support novice principals by assigning experienced secretaries to beginners, or by simply inviting people to call the central offices with any questions about local operating procedures or policies. Then, too, when people take their first principalships after a few years of serving as assistant principals, they often have built a fairly strong repertoire of managerial skills while working with one or more experienced principals. What even very seasoned assistant principals typically do not know is how it feels to be in the top administrative position in a school—the real "hot seat."

Mentoring for beginning principals is a desirable practice. However, such a practice works best if it is directed largely at supporting first-year administrators in their efforts to increase their skill levels in the areas of socialization and self-awareness of new jobs in a new school system. Such mentoring ideally focuses on the needs and feelings of individuals during the first year of service as administrators.

The establishment of mentoring relationships will not automatically guide you through a successful first year. Having a thoughtful and caring mentor will certainly help, but you have to be committed to doing things on your own as well. Understanding that different groups of people have different expectations of what you are supposed to do is extremely important. At this point in your career, you probably believe that the most critical tasks for principals to perform are to take care of the technical and managerial side of the job—maintain the budget and schedule, keep your school building clean and neat, keep within the law, and so on. These are certainly important things for any principal to do.

However, it is also important to note that your colleague principals will expect other behaviors from you. Other principals in your district expect "new folks" to be good colleagues—people who fit in with them and contribute to the well-being of the school district in general. Superintendents want principals who are self-confident—people who believe that they can do the job for which they were hired. The research findings suggest that you will not be viewed by others as very successful if you spend all your time taking care of business in your school. Others expect that you can do the job according to the district's published job description. They want you to add your own personality and ability to the quality of life in your new professional home. That may be one of the reasons why a lot of beginning principals are shocked to find out that they are not evaluated highly by their own school systems, even when they have spent a lot of time in their own buildings doing the job they believe they were hired to do.

Most of the advice in this chapter is directed toward the need to remain attentive to the alternative expectations of professional peers and supervisors in the school district. These relationships are, of course, always important. However, you cannot forget that, in these days of increased emphasis on accountability to the public, there are also other key actors whose perceptions and expectations need to be heard and understood. Private business concerns look to the public schools as a source of future workers who will be well-prepared to step in to take both hourly labor jobs and also management and technical jobs. As a principal, you must ensure that effective instructional and curricular practices meet those goals. Parents, of course, want schools to do other things. Schools should represent safe and secure environments where students learn basic skills that will be needed to achieve future personal, academic, and professional goals and objectives. Principals are expected, therefore, to oversee safe schools where children are challenged and learn. Finally, we often tend to forget that students have expectations of schools and principals. They want to learn and be able to engage in activities that lead to satisfaction and increased self-esteem. They also seek enjoyable interpersonal relationships. And above all, they seek respect from peers and adults. Principals must be aware of all of these and other expectations and remind themselves continuously that they are, in fact, leaders of learners, not simply managers of school buildings.

One additional word of explanation and perhaps caution is worth mentioning. Although research has found that various groups look differently at the relative importance of skills that need to be demonstrated by beginning principals, no individual items or categories of skills (managerial and technical, socialization, or self-awareness) are totally unimportant. Every item on the survey was viewed as critical. However, when faced with a need to prioritize, different groups find certain items more critical than others. Although information presented here is meant to guide you and give you some notion of how other educators view your job, in large measure, how you personally view your job and its various responsibilities and tasks must be a matter for you to define on your own. Once again, it is critical to understand and remain consistent with your own personal and professional platforms as a way to guide your decisions in this area. More information regarding this information activity is provided in a later chapter.

YOUR PERSONAL PLAN

This chapter concludes by asking you to incorporate the ideas and concepts learned in these pages into your personal professional portfolio as a way to guide your growth as a principal. Now that you have had the opportunity to think about the kinds of skills that you value, as seen by your responses to the Beginning Principal's Critical Skills Inventory and compared with the perceptions of others, where do you believe is the greater degree of difference between what you value and what experienced principals and superintendents appear to value?

_____

_____

_____

_____

If you were to ask a sample of parents to complete the skills survey, which items do you believe they would rank as most important? Least important? What are the greatest differences between your views and those of parents of students in your school?

_____

_____

_____

_____

In what areas do you find the greatest similarities and overlaps between your assumptions and the assumptions of experienced principals, superintendents, and perhaps parents and others who have an interest in schools and the work of principals?

_____

_____

_____

_____

In the space below, note some of the ways in which you plan to address the differences between your perceptions of most critical skills and the perceptions of your colleagues and others.

_____

_____

_____

_____

10

Learning Your School's Culture

Ed Walsh was excited on this, his first day as the new principal of Benito Juarez Elementary School. Although he had three years of experience as a junior high school assistant principal in a nearby community, he had always looked forward to the day when he would have his own building. He had always wanted to step into a setting where he would have the chance to implement some of the ideas he had for creating more effective ways to help early adolescents. Ed had been a very successful middle school teacher for several years. He enjoyed a reputation as a very dedicated and innovative teacher. It was not surprising that he now saw a chance to carry out a lot of his dreams through his new role as the leader of a school. He would be the instructional leader of Benito Juarez.

Ed was thinking of the many things he wanted to do to change the school's curriculum and instructional practices as he walked into his office for the first time as principal in July. Of course, he had been in the school before, when he came for the interview and also when the superintendent took him for a walk-through before the school board formally approved his appointment. On both occasions, he looked but really didn't see much. He had been so excited about the things he planned to do as the new principal that now he couldn't recall many of the details of his new school's physical plant. It was a bit like the experience that he and his wife had many years ago when they bought their first home. A few hours after they signed their offer to buy the house, they realized that they knew very little about the details of what they had just purchased. All they knew was it was their first house—their home—and they were happy. Ill-fitting closet doors and a few cracks on the basement floor were lost in their immediate enthusiasm.

Ed looked around his new office at Benito Juarez and noticed that it was a large room with a nice pair of windows that looked out onto the playground. He also realized that the room was extremely hot—a fact that he hadn't recognized when the superintendent took him through the building late last Monday evening. An air conditioner had been installed by the last principal, but Ed didn't plan to use it much. He really didn't mind the heat. After all, he didn't plan to spend that much time in his office anyway. And besides that, this was his school!

Ed also noted two additional features of his office that he hadn't paid much attention to before taking the keys. First, a large bookcase covered one wall. It was filled with books and manuals left by the previous principal, who hadn't been back to collect all his personal belongings since he transferred to another school in the district. Ed looked at the titles of the materials left on the shelves. In addition to the expected items, such as the district policy manual and the district elementary school curriculum guides, all the other reading material dealt with either classroom management techniques or approaches to student discipline.

What concerned Ed more were the two study carrels that faced another wall in his office. When he asked his secretary why they were being stored in his office, she smiled and said they weren't being stored there; they were part of the furnishings that had been there as long as the previous principal had been at Benito Juarez. These study carrels were used in the in-school suspension program. The principal personally supervised students placed on ISS, as it was called in the district.

Ed made a mental note to box up the books and call the former principal that afternoon. He had a custodian move the carrels out into the hallway so they could be taken to the central office warehouse for storage. Ed didn't plan on being the in-school suspension monitor. He was going to be an instructional leader, not a cop!

Start out by describing the principal of Benito Juarez Elementary School before Ed Walsh came on board.

_____

_____

_____

_____

The description of Ed's predecessor may include terms such as "strict," "attentive to discipline," "unwilling to go out of his office very much," and even "uninvolved with instructional practices." These might be very unfair generalizations concerning a person's entire professional career or presence in a particular school. For example, it is quite possible that teachers who used to work with the principal might use different terms, such as "he really cared about the kids," "he never interfered with our work," and even, "he had his priorities right by placing the teachers' need to work with kids who wanted to learn ahead of other less important things." The carrels for student discipline, the nature of the books, and the fact that the principal's office was air conditioned while the rest of the school was not contribute to an image of what the former building administrator did. It does not mean that what took place in the past was necessarily bad. The fact that the previous principal was at Benito Juarez for several years probably means that the way he approached his job was viewed by many as quite effective.

This points to an important issue that a new principal needs to address, namely, how to reconcile his or her new ways of approaching the principalship with those of the last principal. It is important for the newcomer to ask, "What did the staff expect of the last principal?" because in most cases, what was expected in the past will likely define what is expected of the new principal.

In the case of Ed Walsh at Benito Juarez Elementary School, what are likely to be some of the expectations that the staff has of a principal who steps in after the person who personally kept track of ISS students and maintained a strong emphasis on student discipline in the school?

_____

_____

_____

_____

Once again, it is impossible to say absolutely what images the teachers at Benito Juarez all had of the role of the principal. But it looks like many people may have thought that the last person was good because he took care of the "bad boys and girls" so the teachers wouldn't be bothered by that sort of problem. The former principal appears to not have spent much time out in the school, in teachers' classes, or otherwise relating to the staff. Instead, he stayed in his office and responded to the needs of most of his teachers by making certain that the school was calm, orderly, and well-disciplined. Teachers could teach effectively because the principal took care of all the trouble, and the principal appeared comfortable in that role. After all, his professional library reflected a serious interest in learning about student discipline and behavior management.

Ed Walsh may be in for quite a shock when his teachers return from their summer vacation and find the study carrels gone from the principal's office and the new principal out in the halls, visiting classrooms and observing teachers all day long. "How will the new guy be able to do what Mr. X used to do?" will be a popular question heard in the faculty lounge. The next few weeks, or even months, will represent a very difficult transition period in which teachers will need to recognize that the old principal is gone and, more important, so is the old image of what a principal is supposed to do to help teachers. Ed could be in for a rough time if he does not appreciate these subtle but critical issues. I am not advocating the maintenance of the old system and image for no reason other than to make teachers comfortable. Quite the contrary; change is often needed, and the new principal has been hired largely to bring about change. But it is critical that a newcomer realize what existed in the past, who the heroes were, what are some of the shared war stories of the school, and then celebrate that history and move cautiously into the future.

DON'T JUST LOOK . . . SEE

The school you have just inherited has a lot of important signs that you need to be able to see if you are going to understand the culture, appreciate it, celebrate it, and then move on. Ed Walsh could have been in for a terrible first year if he had *looked* at the book titles and study carrels and had not *seen* what they truly represented. On the one hand, what was present was clutter and some other principal's books in a small office. Taking time to *see* might enable a principal like Ed to appreciate the culture, history, symbols, and, in general, values and expectations of a community.

What did you know about the culture of your school before you came to work there? (Note: If you are working as the principal in a school where you formerly served as a teacher or in some other capacity, is your view of the school the same as it was in the past? Why or why not?)

_____

_____

_____

_____

List some of the things you saw when you first came to your present school that impressed you as signs of "the way they do things around here."

_____

_____

_____

_____

What did you do in response to the things you saw?

_____

_____

_____

_____

Who were some of the heroes in your school? Why were they so important to people?

_____

_____

_____

_____

When a newcomer first arrives, it is critical that he or she spends time looking very carefully at the whole environment to see what story is being told. It is also an important exercise for teachers who think they know their school but will have a new and different perspective if they return to their schools in a different role (i.e., as a principal). For example, did the former principal arrange his or her desk in a way that served as a kind of barrier to people who came into the office? Are the classrooms reflective of a lot of informal teaching settings for small group discussion, or does it appear that the preferred mode of instruction is very formal, lecture-style classroom arrangements? If so, what might these signs suggest about the climate or feel of the school in which you now work? What do you see in the teachers' rooms? Is there evidence of a lot of kidding around or joking that seems to be a part of how the teachers interact? Did you see your office decorated in your predecessor's belongings, or are there any examples of the teachers' relationship with "the boss?" For example, are there such things as gag gifts, cartoon clips, or memory books provided by the staff? What about souvenirs given to the principal by the students (e.g., a baseball signed by all the players on last year's team, or a photo of the band at a recent competition, and so forth)?

The critical issue here is that "a school is not a school is not. . . ." Each building, regardless of size, location, level of students served, geographic site, and just about any other variable selected, has a completely different reality, history, or feel about it. Like individual people, schools have different personalities. Often, these personalities are easier to identify than one might assume. If the newcomer takes time to see the subtle signs of the system, rather than quickly looking things over, the reality of a school will become apparent.

Don't forget, too, that you need to be able to identify what many call the informal organization of your school. This refers to the people and things that don't have formal titles but influence what goes on in your school each day. Informal leaders of your school, or key individuals, need to be recognized as soon as possible. Also, take time to learn about the subcultures in your school. Many people make a huge mistake by walking into a school and assuming that all teachers are one group, the secretaries and clerks are another group, and so on. Factions exist, and loyalties appear from one small group to another. For example, some of your teachers may be ardent supporters of the local teachers' association or union who went out on the picket lines during a recent strike. Other teachers may have been vehemently opposed to such activity. Some custodians may have sided with the strikers, whereas others did not.

LISTEN . . . DON'T JUST HEAR

The importance of seeing a school and not simply looking at it is similar to taking time to listen to what is happening in a school. It is important to remain attentive to the sounds and language of your new environment. They provide many subtle indications of the culture, climate, and informal organization in which you now work.

Listen carefully to the words that the teachers use to describe the students. Are they filled with warmth and support? Or do they express a constant battle between "us" and "them?" Do the war stories shared in the teachers' lounge reflect instances of adults controlling kids ("You should have seen how I scared them into shaping up last period."), or are the stories shared about successes in achieving positive results? ("My third period English class was really great this morning. You should have seen the presentations they made!") Of course, most schools will have a mixture of both kinds of teacher talk. But in some schools, the prevailing philosophy of the teachers in relation to their work with students is visible and needs to be recognized (if not necessarily endorsed) by a new principal. One of the challenges that a principal may face involves changing staff attitudes toward children. But changes cannot take place on the first day, and ignoring past attitudes will not help the change process.

How would you describe the context and tone of the teacher talk about students and other issues in your school?

_____

_____

_____

_____

Another important indicator of your new school is what you hear in your office from secretaries, clerks, custodians, nurses, cafeteria workers, and all the staff members that are described as your "Invisible Heroes" in Chapter 7. Also, you need to gain insights into the general public and parents and their expectations for what your school should "look like." Any new principal would do well to listen attentively to the tone of language (friendly and cordial, or too businesslike and cold?) that people use with individuals from outside the school. Have you ever called a business on the phone and then decided to go somewhere else simply because of the way you were addressed? People experience the same feelings when they call a school.

If you knew nothing about your school other than the sound of your secretary's voice, what impressions might you have of your building?

_____

_____

_____

_____

Another thing that listening to subtle sounds in your school will tell you very quickly is the degree of formality that exists in the building in which you have recently become the principal. Do teachers call you by your first name, or do they tend to refer to you more formally? (Take note: Use the same format when you address them.) How do they refer to each other? It is not surprising to hear teachers who have worked with each other for many years continue to use formal terms in addressing each other ("Mrs. Garcia" or "Mr. Jones"), at least during the course of the school day. Often this is particularly true in big city schools. This may surprise you, but honor it and repeat it. Some practices will never die; calling Mrs. Johnson "Sara" in front of her students may be offensive and may distance you and a teacher who might otherwise become one of your strongest allies.

Walk through the halls of your school and listen to the sounds you hear, the sounds coming out of teachers' classrooms. Is there a lot of good-natured laughing or a considerable amount of angry, raised voices indicating that teachers are spending a lot of time disciplining their students? Or is it extremely quiet? Any of these signs may be indicative of the general tone of your school.

If a person who knew little about your school walked through the halls one day and listened, what kind of general impressions of the school would he or she take away?

_____

_____

_____

_____

CELEBRATE THE PAST

A natural, almost unavoidable contradiction presents itself when a new principal walks into a school. The new leader is almost always expected to do something different, bring about change of one sort or another, and "make a difference." But school are very fragile and normally very conservative organizations. "The way we've always done things" is a pretty strong front that people seek to maintain. Thus, the new principal might be criticized for not doing enough but also for trying to do too much at the same time.

Consider the dilemma facing Ed Walsh. He knew that the district hired him because they really wanted some strong instructional leaders. But he noticed that his predecessor had been primarily an office-bound disciplinarian. If he didn't bring about change and assert himself in one way, he would get into trouble with the central office and school board. On the other hand, when he threw out the carrels and said he would no longer take on discipline as his primary, defining activity, his teachers were upset. What was he to do?

The fictional Ed Walsh is patterned on a principal who now has more than 15 years of experience as an administrator, the first 10 years of which were at "Benito Juarez Elementary School," where he was respected by his teachers and central office staff as well. However, if someone could invent a magical instrument called a "retrospectoscope" to allow one to look backward and do things differently in the future, it would be possible to second-guess things that made his beginning as a principal more difficult than it needed to be.

Perhaps the most significant thing that Ed did that may have made his arrival at his new home a bit more troublesome was the fact that he did not talk to any of his new staff members about their perceptions of why the former principal did some of the things that he did. Ed had the right to change the image of the principalship from one of chief disciplinarian to instructional leader. In fact, his efforts ought to be commended. But when he simply took steps to remove any sign of his predecessor from the school, he was symbolically denying something that many of his teachers did not feel comfortable about losing. Even if many teachers did not like the former principal, Ed's actions seemed to suggest that the teachers and the former principal were wrong. At the very least, it was important for Ed to share with several teachers what he planned to do. He could have assured them that he was not going to discredit any of the fine work done in the past. Rather, he was simply trying to start things off with the perspective of the "new kid on the block."

Another thing that Ed could have done shortly after the beginning of the new school year was to invite the former principal to drop by and visit his old school and talk about some of his visions for Benito Juarez. In addition, some discussions about the history, culture, and traditions of the school could help both the new and the former principal develop additional insights into the school, teachers, students, and community.

Do you have any additional suggestions for how the shift from one principal to the next could be made less traumatic?

_____

_____

_____

_____

It is critical that new principals not charge into their new settings so forcefully that they forget to honor the past. Former staff members, practices, policies, and traditions might need to be replaced, but they also need to be publicly respected because they represent many subtle aspects of life in an organization. Any newly arrived administrator who does not celebrate the good work of the past will have many unnecessary battles with people who might see the newcomer as disrespectful, unfeeling, or insensitive to the local culture. By the same token, remember that one of the things that a new leader needs to do is assess the practices of the past and determine what was viewed negatively by parents, teachers, and others. Simply wanting to avoid the appearance of getting rid of all past practices does not mean that you must be bound to repeat undesirable work as well.

DEVELOP AN ACTION PLAN

Describe the most important aspects of the school culture that you inherited as the new principal, that is, the kinds of things you must understand as you step in as the new leader.

_____

_____

_____

_____

Which elements of the past culture represent things you cannot comfortably live with as the new principal?

_____

_____

_____

_____

What practices appear to have been popular with faculty, students, and parents? Why?

_____

_____

_____

_____

How do you plan to step away from the past practices in a way that will not alienate you from your staff or other important people in your school environment?

_____

_____

_____

_____

How do you hope to replace the things that you are not comfortable with in your new school? Why?

_____

_____

_____

_____

What are some of the features of your new school that you believe should be maintained as much as possible? Why?

_____

_____

_____

_____

PART III

Self-Awareness

Although the technical and managerial skills and socialization are important issues for the beginning principal to deal with, self-awareness may be the single most crucial concern for those who are stepping on board as administrators. The next chapters focus on some ways you may be able to relate your own values and perspectives to what it means to be a leader of a school.

11

Reviewing Personal Values

Beginning principals experience difficulties during their first year on the job for many reasons. In some cases, they do not take care of business. For example, they might ignore the importance of completing assigned administrative tasks on time, or they might violate local policies or even state laws. Another reason for getting into trouble is that they do not seem to have the kinds of people skills needed to communicate effectively with parents, staff, other administrators, or even students. Experienced personnel or human resource administrators have often noted that two sure ways for a principal to lose his or her job are mismanagement of the budget and school finances (technical or managerial skill) or engaging in indiscreet personal contact with teachers, staff members, parents, or particularly sadly, students. In recent news stories, it is increasingly clear that communities will have no tolerance for any school administrator who "looks the other way" when teachers or staff members have improper relationships with students. Administrators are viewed as responsible for outrageous behaviors in their schools and are likely to suffer severe consequences in most cases.

In this chapter, however, the focus is on yet another area found to be a serious problem for many beginning principals. Research on beginning leadership problems identifies the importance of people coming to grips with their own set of personal and professional values and priorities as they develop self-awareness skills, as described in Chapter 2.

This chapter suggests a strategy that might be used to identify important personal and professional values before walking into the principal's office for the first time.

CASE: BECAUSE IT'S IMPORTANT TO ME

Lionel Spencer, principal at Thomas Jefferson High School, was in trouble. He had just gotten a call from Dr. Moira Kingsley, assistant superintendent for administrative services. She pointed out to Lionel that for the fourth month in a row, he was at least one week late in turning in his Building Use Report Plan (BURP) to the central office. According to Dr. Kingsley, this was an important form because it provided a good deal of information regarding the ways Thomas Jefferson and the other high schools in the district were being used by community groups in the evenings and on weekends. This, in turn, could be used in the superintendent's monthly report to the community to show how responsive the schools were to public needs and interests. And with an important bond election (and possible extension of the superintendent's contract) coming up in about six months, it was critical for the district to talk to the voters.

Lionel offered his apologies, again, to Dr. Kingsley and promised to get last month's report to her as soon as possible and make sure that he got this month's report to her on time. As soon as he hung up the phone, however, he looked at his calendar for the next three days and realized that it would be virtually impossible to find the time to fill in the BURP report. Class visits were scheduled for the remainder of today. Lionel had promised his teachers that he would visit each teacher's classroom whenever the teacher felt the principal could be of assistance in that way. Furthermore, Anne Marie Burkowitz, the assistant principal, had made a similar commitment to be on call for supervisory assistance. The secretaries in Lionel's office were overloaded with work associated with the upcoming regional accreditation visit. And both Lionel and Anne Marie were going to be tied up the next three nights with different activities at the school. The boys' basketball game against archrival Woodrow Wilson was tonight, there was a wrestling match tomorrow night, and there was a parent advisory committee meeting on the next night. Tomorrow's schedule was also filled with classroom observations, and Lionel also knew that a certain percentage of his time would be devoted to responding to whatever momentary problems walked into his office each day.

Lionel knew within a minute after talking with Dr. Kingsley that he would be hearing from her again in a few days. But he also knew that he was doing the best job he knew how to do, whether he met the expectations of the central office administrators or not.

CASE: BUT WHAT ABOUT THE CHILDREN?

Mary Carmody had worked her way up through several different roles in the San Juan schools during her career. She started as a primary grades teacher, then served as an at-risk coordinator for two years. She moved to a position in the central office as a parent liaison for another year, but she really missed the action at the school site level. Four years ago, she became the assistant principal at the Mission Viejo Elementary School, one of the poorest schools in the entire San Juan school district. She quickly became known in that role. She had met many of the more active parents from Mission when she worked at the central office. She also had the gift of being fluent in Spanish, a fact that had helped her many times in her career in this community located directly on the U.S.-Mexico border. These things all contributed to her reputation as someone who could "really get out in the community to work with families."

When the principalship opened up at Simon Fernandez Elementary, a virtual twin school to Mission Viejo located only about a mile down the street, there was little doubt that Mary would be named the new campus leader. From the first day on the job at Fernandez, Mary was visited by what seemed to be an endless stream of visitors from the neighborhood who had heard that this principal could be trusted as a true *amiga* to the community.

Shortly after the October school census reports were completed, Mary was visited by Yvette Calderon, her school's attendance clerk. Yvette came into Mary's office with several pages of student residence information, closed the door, and began to share her concerns with the principal. "Ms. Carmody, we have a big problem. I started reviewing this information while I was putting together the census reports two weeks ago, and I started to notice some very strange things. A lot of our kids all seem to live in the same apartment building over on Chestnut Street. At least that's what their addresses on file with us suggest. I sent Manny Escobar, the district attendance officer for our area, over to Chestnut to check on this. He came back yesterday and told me that there is no way that all these kids can be living in that building. He says it is just a "front" for kids who live in Mexico and want to come to the U.S. for schools."

Mary knew that this situation existed across the district. She knew from her past experience at Mission Viejo, and from working with parents across the district, it was likely that a large percentage of the children at Fernandez were undocumented aliens living in Mexico but returning early each morning to attend schools in the United States. From a legal and financial perspective, this was indeed a bad situation. Legally, Mexican children could attend schools in San Juan, but their parents were expected to pay tuition to the district. Indeed, there were many children in the district who were tuition-paying nonresidents. However, most of the students who did so came from affluent families in Mexico. The kids attending Fernandez certainly did not fit that description. Most came from substandard housing across the border. Nevertheless, Mary asked her attendance clerk to check on whether the suspected nonresidents were, in fact, attending the school under false pretenses.

A few days later, Yvette returned to Mary's office. "I checked all the records. Of the 40 students I suspected, only two of them are legal residents of the district. That means we have at least 38 students who shouldn't be here. Should I call Pupil Services to start the paperwork to remove these kids from our roster?"

"No. Give me some time to think this one out. There's more than tuition money to be lost here," said Mary.

Now the responsibility was truly on the principal's shoulders. She knew that there were several students who were illegally enrolled at the school. At the same time, Mary had seen many of the *escuelas primeras* that these children would be attending in Mexico. Based on her different experiences with parents, poverty, at-risk students, and just living her whole life here on the border, Mary Carmody knew that enforcing a district policy here would likely destroy most of these children's hopes for a very different future. At the same time, Mary was a taxpayer and had no interest in putting her career in jeopardy by ignoring a policy and the law. She knew the next day or two would involve a lot of second guessing on her part.

School principals make hundreds of decisions every day. Each is made through certain lenses that the individual brings to the job, and the sources of these lenses are varied. Some come from written school board policy manuals. For example, a principal quickly decides that a secretary is entitled to take next Friday off to go to a doctor's appointment because the school district has a rather clear statement of what constitutes sick leave or personal leave. These are easy decisions to make in most cases. Principals are called upon to make other decisions, and many times these are not easy matters; the issues and "correct" answers are not easily defined and are not readily made according to the written policy of the school system.

Consider, for example, decisions such as the one that Lionel Spencer had to make in the first case study above. Lionel had to decide whether he would comply with the requirements of the school district and fill out his monthly report or use his limited time in other ways. What is the deciding factor? Lionel's personal and professional values have a lot to do with his ultimate choice (and also the probable consequences resulting from his decisions). Lionel Spencer valued contact with his teachers and students more than he did a paper report. No printed manual or other material guided his choice.

The decision facing Mary is also one that has to be ultimately based on personal goals and values. The consequences of her choice are likely to be far greater than simply not getting another report done so that the superintendent could brag about building usage in the district. Instead, one choice made by the principal could result in less effective education for many children. The other choice might result in the misuse of public funds and a serious breach of district policy. Mary's case description ends purposefully without a definite resolution, to note that some decisions that we make are truly almost "lose-lose" in nature, even when most leadership analysts might suggest that all decisions should result in "win-win" outcomes for all concerned. But the fact is that there are times when no answer is completely appealing or "correct."

Most decisions made by principals are truly matters of personal choice. In many cases, the reasons principals use in making their decisions are unclear to an outside observer. Mrs. Jones gets to take her class on a field trip, but Mr. Smith is not permitted to go. Bobby Wilson is given three days of in-school suspension for using inappropriate language in talking back to a teacher, but Mary Pierce is simply reprimanded for what appears to be the same offense and is sent back to the classroom. Teachers complain about what they believe are inconsistencies in the behaviors of principals. Yet, principals often do not seem concerned about what others believe are differential patterns in their behavior. However, experienced principals have learned—often the hard way—that differences in perceptions, whether they are right or wrong, represent real beliefs and views of others. As a consequence, these perceptions must be understood, appreciated, and addressed.

Chapter 2 discussed the importance of developing a strong sense of self-awareness as a critical skill for beginning principals. Remember that of all the behavior noted by superintendents, the most valued was the ability to show clearly one's personal beliefs and values and recognize why one was selected for a leadership role in the first place. Incidentally, it will be interesting to see whether Lionel's superintendent changes his rating of Lionel when the BURP report is late again! Will Mary survive if it is discovered that she chose to overlook the presence of large numbers of students who should have been denied access to free education in her school?

Awareness of one's duties and responsibilities in a job comes about largely as the product of a reflective process in which one constantly matches the requirements of the job with a personal value system. The more a person is content with the most important attitudes, values, and beliefs that drive a person, the happier he or she will be—and the more effective, productive, and ultimately, successful. It is a simple fact that when a person becomes more invested in a job as a personal commitment, he or she will not only be more satisfied, but more effective as well.

One way to review one's personal value and belief system as it relates to the realities of the job of the principalship is by a periodic review of a personal educational platform. A platform is a philosophical statement, although I avoid the term "philosophical" because most practicing administrators stay away from things that are too philosophical or theoretical. A platform statement puts into writing some of the nearest and dearest beliefs that a person might have about the educational issues that define a major part of his or her work life. It is often said that the major planks in a platform express an individual's nonnegotiable values. In many ways, they represent the core values of a person—if they are violated by the nature of the job one has to do or other factors, it may be reasonable to think about leaving the job.

Finally, a statement of a personal platform has the potential either (a) to guide a person away from a professional role that is viewed as inconsistent with personal values, or simply (b) to enable a person to know when a particular placement in a job is not what was envisioned in the first place. For example, a platform can help a person recognize whether selecting the principalship as a career goal was a good choice, or whether taking a particular principalship in a specific community was the best move. In either case, if the personal values that are expressed in a platform are not attainable in a job in one location, it may be reasonable to move on.

BUILDING A PLATFORM

In the pages that follow, I will lead you through the development of an educational platform. Many different approaches might be followed in carrying out this exercise. You are invited to modify anything offered here so that it is more consistent with your own needs, interests, and, of course, personal values.

You will be asked several questions that have to do with the central issues faced by educators, in most cases regardless of whether they work in classrooms or administrative offices. After each question, space is provided for you to write down your responses. Simply filling in the blanks does not necessarily mean that you have prepared a philosophical statement that might cause you to quit a job.

A personal educational platform has the power of putting on paper the bottom line of an individual educator. Your answers below might serve as an important foundation for a more cohesive statement that you will craft at some point in the future.

1. What is the purpose of schooling?

People have struggled with this issue for almost as long as there have been formal organizations called schools. Is it your view that students attend these formal organizations to acquire vocational skills? For moral development? To develop basic skills primarily? To learn about good citizenship and other values related to life in a democratic society? Perhaps other purposes guide your vision, as noted below.

_____

_____

_____

_____

2. What are the key ingredients of an "adequate" education for all students?

There has been a lot of talk about how to get schools back to the basics. Although this phrase has become a kind of slogan for a particular conservative point of view regarding schooling, each educator must have some sense of what the basic elements of good schooling might include.

_____

_____

_____

_____

3. What is the appropriate role for students?

Perhaps an even more important issue to be considered here concerns one's personal view of who students are. It is widely assumed that educators all have a core value that speaks to the needs of pupils as the driving force in schools. Although this may sound appealing and "right," is it truly your vision or value?

_____

_____

_____

_____

4. What is the appropriate role for teachers?

Again, the question might revolve around your personal definition of what teachers are in the first place. Some people view teachers as true professionals who have the best interests of their students in mind as they proceed with their duties. Others view teachers as district employees who can be replaced easily with others who happen to have the same certification and academic degrees. Are these views compatible with your perspective, or do you have other notions of who teachers are and what they should be doing in schools?

_____

_____

_____

_____

5. What is the appropriate role for parents and other community members?

Most schools greet visitors with signs or decals on the front door with a statement such as "This is your school and welcome to it." But do you mean that? Are parents truly partners in the educational program or are they intruders? What about the great majority of community members out there who pay taxes but who do not have children enrolled in your (or any other) public school? What about your views of private businesses in your community?

_____

_____

_____

_____

6. What is my personal definition of "curriculum?"

Modern definitions of effective principals note that they are instructional, or curricular, leaders. What does this mean in practice? Part of it must be based on one's ability to have a clear personal understanding of what the curriculum is and what it should be in a particular school setting. For example, how inclusive shall a school's curriculum be?

_____

_____

_____

_____

7. What do I want this school to become?

What is your personal vision for the school? What kinds of hopes and dreams for a more effective school drive your work? What are your ideals?

_____

_____

_____

_____

8. How will I know if students learned?

The ultimate goal of any school must be to ensure that learning has taken place among students. But what are the indicators, at least in your mind, of whether this has really taken place? Some say that students' score on standardized achievement tests are valid indicators, whereas others say learning really occurs only when established outcomes or performances are reached. What is your answer?

_____

_____

_____

_____

9. How do I want others to see me?

It is important for a leader to reflect on the kind of image that he or she projects to followers. How do you hope you will be viewed by your teachers, staff, students, parents, and community members? Think about this issue in two ways, as a principal and also as a private citizen.

_____

_____

_____

_____

10. What are my nonnegotiable values?

This last question might be the single most important issue to be addressed in your platform. Ultimately, this question asks you to consider the kinds of things that, if violated by the system or by other people with whom you must work, would cause you to throw your keys on the table and seek employment elsewhere.

_____

_____

_____

_____

WHAT DO YOU DO WITH THE PLATFORM?

The value of an educational platform is not found by simply writing it out one time, putting it in a file cabinet, and then letting it sit there for the rest of your professional life. Rather, it should be seen as a living document or statement regarding the parameters that you will put around different decisions made in your career. Platforms will change as you move through your professional life. For example, your thinking about the desirability of standardized testing as a way to measure student growth and progress may change drastically from day to day until some point in the future. Your vision of "perfect teachers" may be modified greatly as you move further away from your days in that role.

The development of a formal statement of values through the educational platform has many important applications that can be of great assistance to you as you travel through your career as an educational leader. For one thing, developing clarity regarding your nonnegotiable values—even though these might change in the future—can be a genuine help to you as you think about changing jobs, moving to other districts, accepting transfers within your school system, and so on. For example, I know many colleagues who have turned their backs on higher salaries and more prestigious jobs because taking these jobs would cause them to compromise nonnegotiable values, such as being able to stay home more with their families or continuing to work with students from populations that need attention.

Second, the articulation of a clear statement of an educational platform is of value to those with whom you are to work, both at your individual school site and across your district. It isn't a good idea to print multiple copies of your platform and then send them around to everyone you might meet! However, people who have taken the time to write their platforms from time to time inevitably have a stronger grasp of their own values, so that those around them are also able to see what makes them tick. This not only has the benefit of enabling principals to be open to their staffs, but it is also a very powerful way to model communications skills that lead to more effective schooling in general. In the long run, becoming more clear about your personal educational values will assist you when you seek other professional positions. For example, an opening for a principalship in another school district that seems more prestigious or offers a higher salary might not be nearly as desirable once you consider the possible compromises that might be needed with regard to your personal values.

Finally, the ultimate value of developing a clear statement of an educational platform may be that it can serve as the foundation for long-term professional development. Too often, educators simply drift through their careers and engage in sporadic and periodic programs of professional growth and development based on learning more about one hot topic or another, because the central office has made it clear that "all principals ought to jump on this or that bandwagon." In many cases, principals simply respond to the visions or platforms of others. It would be far more desirable for principals to engage in systematic career planning that is rooted in their own values and sense of where they are going or what is important to learn. For this reason, it is often suggested that people begin their professional development portfolios with a clear statement of their platforms. In that way, other elements of the portfolio are able to flow in a logical sequence from a strong foundation.

YOUR PERSONAL PLATFORM

In the next few pages, sketch out some of the more critical elements of your personal portfolio and growth plan. You may wish to consult and respond to the questions posed earlier, or you may respond to other critical issues that will provide a greater sense of who you are as a professional educator.

_____

_____

_____

_____

Now that you have written the planks of your platform, the last step in this self-improvement process involves a clear statement of what you plan to do to implement your personal vision of effective practice. Once you have completed this last step, a final valuable activity involves sharing your statement with one or two close friends, family members, or colleagues with a simple request that they indicate whether they recognize in you some of what you have written and whether you have written a real or ideal description.

_____

_____

_____

_____

12

Being a "Boss"

Sharon Mitchell was really excited last summer when she got the word that she had been selected as the new principal of O'Hare Elementary School, a small building with a great reputation for effective teachers and very supportive and involved parents. As a teacher for several years at the Midway Elementary School only a few blocks from O'Hare, Sharon had been able to see what was going on in her new school. She was always impressed with the place, and she felt as if she had died and gone to heaven when she learned that her first administrative position would be at O'Hare.

Soon after she moved into her new office in July, Sharon began to realize that being a principal did indeed carry with it a great deal of responsibility not generally covered in the district policy manual or established job description. Furthermore, she saw quickly that the courses she had completed for state principal certification at Meigs University had not really provided her with a complete picture of her new school or her job as a principal.

For example, she quickly understood that now that she was the principal, people reacted to her quite differently. She had known most of the teachers at O'Hare for many years. But now, as they began to come to their classrooms for the start of the new school year, she could feel a distinct chill in the air. She was now "Mrs. Mitchell" to many who had referred to her simply as "Sharon" in the past. Also, it now seemed like a major production just to get out of her building at the same time each day so she could get home to prepare dinner for her family, a task she now looked forward to simply because it reminded her of a time when she could get something accomplished in a predictable way. And the smiling folks at central office who said so many supportive things during the job interview were beginning to make it clear that she would be treated like all the other principals in the district, despite the fact that most other administrators had at least six years of experience.

Finally, Sharon was becoming weary of the seemingly endless parade of parents and other community members who were coming to her door daily with "just one more simple question" or request—often issues and requests that had been denied by the former principal. But Sharon was new on the scene, and many people wanted to test her resolve about a variety of issues.

The school year had just begun, and Sharon was not completely certain that she would make it to Halloween!

When people step into their first principalships, the reaction and situation are often not very different from the scenario described above. Being named as a school principal may be the fulfillment of a long-standing ambition. The conditions associated with a particular position might be quite favorable: the location of the school, an individual's feeling of comfort with the school, the reputation of the teachers, and so on. Even with all these factors going the right way, however, it is impossible to ignore that when you become a principal for the first time, you will face certain issues. One of these is that people will look at you differently, expect different things from you, and hold you accountable in ways that will be markedly different from what they did in the past. Simply stated, you are now "the boss," and this designation carries certain challenges and demands. Once again, this fact reinforces the demand described in earlier chapters, namely, that beginners must recognize that the job of principal is related to your sense of self.

No matter how well-prepared you may feel as you move into a formal leadership role for the first time, it is impossible to escape the fact that being a boss brings with it certain challenges and demands. This chapter will identify some of the challenges that any newcomer is likely to face during the first part of the transition into the principal's office. If you have already served as an assistant principal, you probably have some insights into these issues, although there is still no substitute for serving as the top administrator in a school. When the weight of full responsibility for an organization falls on your shoulders, it is very different from serving as an assistant.

This chapter also includes some practical hints for helping you to increase your self-awareness and sense of who you are in a new professional role so that you can meet the pressures of leadership with greater confidence.

OTHERS' PERCEPTIONS

As Sharon Mitchell discovered rather quickly, one of the things that changes almost immediately when you become the principal is the way other people tend to see you. Of course, you don't feel a lot different from the way you were just a few weeks ago. Admittedly, you may now be considerably more tired, and you may often feel there are not enough hours in a day to carry out your new job. But down deep, you know that you are still the same person you have been for your whole life. It's just that people around you—teachers, office and custodial staff, parents, and students— perceive you differently. You should not deliberately change, but you need to recognize that the perceptions of others can be powerful forces that will affect you directly or affect the ways in which other people see you. In the long run, these are the kinds of things that will enable you to be more effective as a school principal.

Before I list some of the ways beginning principals are perceived differently by people who work with them, if you are currently in the first year as a principal (or if you talk with people who are now beginning principals), list some of the ways you have noticed people treating the rookie principal differently from the way they did in the past. (For example, do people seem less inclined to talk openly with you about some of their professional concerns now?)

_____

_____

_____

_____

_____

_____

_____

_____

Researchers have noted beginning principals receive signals from teachers, colleague administrators, parents (and other community members), students, and immediate family members that suggest they are somehow different now that they are the boss.

Teachers, even in these days of increased empowerment and efforts to provide opportunities for involvement in decision making, still tend to look forward to someone being "in charge." As a result, the role of the formal school leader may change somewhat in tone (perhaps from "dictator" to "facilitator"). But when you are the principal of a school, people will continue to look at you as a person who will make critical decisions in times of need. What is often difficult to remember, however, is that each teacher has a very strong sense of when there is a time of need. Some staff members will rarely come to you to make decisions for them. On the other hand, every school will have a teacher or two (or more) who will rely on the boss to tell them what should be done about even seemingly insignificant issues. ("Would it be all right for me to open a few windows in my classroom, even though it's raining?")

A second aspect of being a boss concerns the idea expressed by the often-cited sign on President Harry Truman's desk: "The buck stops here." When you are in charge of something, whether it's a small elementary school, a large high school, or a huge school district, you are the person who is ultimately responsible for the effective operation of that organization. You cannot make a mistake and then blame it on someone else. However, there are some principals who tend to attribute any unpopular decision to the fact that "the central office made me do it," or "we have to do it because the state requires it." Such principals are typically not respected by their administrative peers, and they usually are not very effective school leaders.

Another price that novice principals often pay is the loneliness they suddenly feel in their school systems. It is ironic that, in many cases, individuals move into administrative positions within their school systems largely because they are recognized as people with great interpersonal and social skills; their peers like and admire them. Often, they are at the center of professional and social gatherings, leading many to assume that they will carry these skills into the principal's office. Many newcomers are then amazed to find out that, as one new principal observed, they have "crossed the line" separating themselves from their teacher friends when they become a principal. As one principal reported, "Last year, when I was still a teacher and I walked into the teachers' lounge, I was the center of attention and had a chance to talk with everyone. This year, as the principal, I walk into that same lounge and there's a dead silence. Same school, same teachers, same me. But people used to talk with me, but now I know they talk about me."

SO WHAT DO YOU DO?

People will often not understand who you are when you take on the role of the principal; they will react to you in a number of ways, some of which may be quite unproductive. For example, some new principals discover that their teachers are not engaging them in the ways they did in the past, and as a result they begin to build walls and isolate themselves. Soon, principals who adopt this stance begin to spend most of their time in their offices or out of their buildings. A common symptom of this situation involves the principal beginning to view things in terms of "us" (or "me") versus "them" (with "them" meaning "all teachers").

Another behavioral pattern often adopted by principals who sense separation from their teaching staffs is the tendency to internalize everything and make everything their sole responsibility. They stop delegating even small tasks. The result can be very unfortunate as they feel stress increasing because they don't have time to do everything, they have no friends, they can't rely on anyone, and they have no one to help them do their jobs.

A third approach is to take on a deliberately officious stance. Some beginning principals hide behind rules, regulations, policies, procedures, and anything else that might serve to depersonalize their jobs. In this way, they can develop the sense that they are not involved with people who are rejecting them. Their stance is one of coming to work, following rules, avoiding contact whenever possible, and then going home without worrying about the people with whom they work. They tend not to be very happy people on the job, to say the least.

Finally, some new principals deal with their sense of separation from teachers by rejecting their roles as administrators and striving to appear as if they are still part of the teaching team. Although this may not at first sound like a problem—after all, isn't it good to still be a teacher?—some major difficulties will inevitably arise when beginning principals avoid "being a boss." It is important to remember, for example, that a major responsibility of any principal is the evaluation of staff, often with the result being an unhappy decision about a person's career. Although principals should not avoid contact with their teachers only because they may have to evaluate them negatively some day, some distance between teachers and administrators may not be totally undesirable.

The fact is no matter how you may wish to deal with it, the step you have taken from your former life as a teacher into administration automatically means that certain relationships will change and that new expectations and demands will naturally follow you into your new role. But that sort of transition does not have to be traumatic or cause the kinds of negative behaviors I have noted here. As one principal observed a few years back, "When you become a principal you have to remember that you are still a part of the family that you were a member of before. But now, you are the head of that family. Your job now becomes one of doing all that you can do to promote the well-being of everybody. You can't be a buddy, but you must be a friend in the truest sense." Differences do not necessarily mean that you care less for everyone in the family. The trick of administration often is to demonstrate caring about others through the establishment of trust. When you achieve that level of interaction, differences between you (the boss) and teachers (the employees) will begin to disappear. If you want separation, you can find it. On the other hand, if you want effective teamwork, you have to work on that, too, but it can be achieved.

Being in charge of any organization can be stressful and can serve to make a person feel alone and even rejected by others from time to time. This is particularly true when people are promoted from within; one day they work with a group of people, but the next day they are making the same people work for them. Nevertheless, you can reduce the sense of separation, and without resorting to the methods described earlier. Your job is not to agonize over the sense of separation but to promote a sense of unity in your school.

What are some of the ways in which you have addressed the issue of feeling apart from your teachers now that you've crossed the line and become the boss? (For example, some principals promote monthly sharing sessions, or "book talks," as a way to increase collegial communication by inviting teachers to spend a half hour or so talking about the professional concerns they are facing.)

_____

_____

_____

_____

_____

_____

_____

STRATEGIES TO REDUCE ISOLATION

The best way to help reduce your sense of isolation is to make links with key people inside and outside your building.

Inside your building, it is critical that you build bridges with a few key individuals who can serve as sounding boards for you throughout the school year. This is not always an easy task. It is nearly impossible to tell who can be trusted as a confidant when you first walk into a new school. This is particularly true if you are new to the school district and have no clear idea of who the players are. Nevertheless, it is essential to find allies in your immediate environment. If you are in an elementary school or a fairly small secondary school, it is likely that the first person who comes to your mind as a person to be trusted is the secretary for the school. She or he will likely know more about the issues facing your school than just about anyone else you will encounter. However, you must guard against allowing your judgment to be clouded by one person's perceptions. Also, it is possible that well-intentioned conversations about key people in your school might become opportunities for gossip and hearsay. Secretaries have great insights into what is going on in schools. On the other hand, they do not always know all the reasons for people's behavior.

If you happen to work in a school that has assistant principals, these individuals might also serve as members of your inner circle of confidants. There are, of course, some restrictions to this suggestion. For example, finding out that one or more of your assistants was an unsuccessful applicant for your job might make you think twice about that person being an ongoing supporter. Also, you may quickly determine that one of the things you must do in your principalship is to encourage your assistant principals to seek opportunities for professional advancement. It is not uncommon for newly appointed principals to bargain with their superintendents to allow them to select their own assistant principal team before formally accepting the principalship of a school. You may need to hire new members for your team, and the time to do that is typically while you are experiencing a "honeymoon period" as the new principal. Despite any reservations noted here, however, reliance on assistants as sources of important information about your new school can effectively reduce your sense of isolation.

A third potential source of support inside your school are the few teachers with whom you can feel comfortable opening up and sharing some personal concerns. Again, these people will not be visible at first as you move into a school; you will have to spend some time and make an effort to find teachers who can be trusted. Remember, too, that those who come forward in the first few days of your life as an administrator are often the last persons who will be enduring supporters. In this regard, you should rely on experiences that you had as a classroom teacher. Eventually, in every class there are a few students who become close allies of the teacher. The same can be said of the dynamics in any teaching staff that you join. Incidentally, this is one of the places where a firm appreciation and understanding of your personal educational platform will be a critical part of your success. How do you look at teachers, for example? As you think through your response to this question, your solid relationships with a few colleagues will emerge quite naturally.

Finally, as you try to assess key issues and other aspects of the internal realities of your school, do not forget that you will have inherited a structure for operating your school that may be quite helpful. It is likely that committees and task forces are already in place and were formed prior to your arrival. Spending time with members of these groups, often in the role of silent observer, can be an important tool for you as you try to develop a positive and comprehensive picture of what's really going on.

If these types of groups don't already exist, you might think about announcing that you want nominations for staff to serve on a building "Steering Committee" or "Instructional Improvement Committee." As people are identified by others as possible candidates for this work, you will develop a strong core of people with whom you may be able to work on a variety of projects, and you will also likely gain some good insights into which people in your school are perceived by their peers as leaders.

At your present school, who might be included as members of your inner circle of confidants? (Will you include your secretary? Assistant principal? Team or grade leaders? Department chairs? A teacher or two with whom you worked when you were in the classroom?)

_____

_____

_____

_____

_____

_____

YOUR PERSONAL PLAN

Again, the issues we have reviewed in this chapter deal with self-awareness or role awareness skills as one of the concerns of beginning administrators. In the space below, you might wish to write down some of the frustrations that you are experiencing because you are now the boss in your school. These frustrations might be linked to the items identified earlier, or they might be unique concerns related to your first job as a school principal. In either case, you ought to include these issues as part of the process of building your personal portfolio and growth plan. For each item listed as a frustration, you may also indicate some of the ways in which you have been able to cope with it and proceed with your work as an educational leader.

_____

_____

_____

_____

_____

_____

_____

_____

SUGGESTED READING

Evetts, J. (1994). _Becoming a secondary headteacher._ London: Cassell.

Hall, P. A. (2004). _The first year principal._ Lanham, MD: Scarecrow Press.

Tooms, A. (2005). _The rookie's playbook: Insights and dirt for new principals._ Lanham, MD: Scarecrow Press.

Villani, S. (2006). _Mentoring and induction programs that support new principals._ Thousand Oaks, CA: Corwin Press.

13

Building a Personal Timeline for Learning and Development

Stanley Wiznewski was determined not to make the same mistakes that many others had made when they got their first principalships. He knew that other rookies had stepped in with the clear intention of simply "surviving" their first year by sitting back and waiting for things to happen. Stanley believed that as a new principal in a very traditional and conservative school district like Upper Harrington, he had only a very brief honeymoon period—a period of opportunity during which he could make the kinds of changes that would enable his school to rise above the other junior high schools in the district. He was committed to hitting the ground running and pushing hard for reforms in his school.

At the same time, Stanley was aware that as a beginning principal, he had to learn about schools, educational administration practice, how to fit in to his new building and school district, as well as the latest research on effective teaching and learning. As a result, he was rapidly becoming more and more fatigued as the school year wore on. He was beginning to really recognize the fact that, if he didn't watch out, he could easily be burned out before the start of the second half of the school year.

Often when people achieve a major professional goal, such as being hired as a school principal for the first time, they want to accomplish a huge amount in as short a time as possible. Indeed, even some research suggests that when people step into a new leadership role, they have only about 12 to 18 months to change the organization in which they now work (or at least start to bring about significant change). If they wait too long, there is a real likelihood that they will become part of the existing scenery, part of the organization that should be changed. This finding, incidentally, may sound like it is contrary to conventional wisdom that suggests that a new leader should keep a very low profile when first coming on board and do nothing to upset people by trying to make too many changes too quickly. The problem, of course, is that moving too fast as a new leader has serious drawbacks. Change might occur, but the cost to the new person might be more than is reasonable as health begins to fail, personal relationships suffer, and followers get caught up in a hectic pace that cannot be maintained for very long.

As new principals review their personal values, dispositions toward leadership, and actual leadership skills, they will need to develop a plan and a timeline to guide their personal and professional development as leaders. This planning process is the focus of this chapter.

A central theme of this book is that simply being equipped with a collection of survival skills to get you through the first year or two on the job is not enough. Of course, when you take any new job, you have a natural interest in learning how to increase your initial comfort by completing assigned tasks in a competent, timely, and efficient manner. There is a lot of truth in the old saying that you can't be a leader if you get fired. As a result, the emphasis in this book is on what to expect at the start of your career. But avoid the temptation of believing that being "good enough" is an adequate way to look at your career as a school principal. My goal is to assist you in developing a long-term vision of leadership that goes beyond simple survival skills.

This chapter will assist you in setting up personal guidelines that you might follow as you journey from being a rookie to eventual status as a veteran educational leader in your present—or some other—school system.

A DEVELOPMENTAL FRAMEWORK

One point needs to be recognized very quickly. As a beginner, you want to do a good job, and the job that you have selected as a career is a big one. There may be a strong tendency for you to want to do a lot of things right away and make certain that everything that you do is a resounding success. After all, the superintendent and school board that hired you probably told you on numerous occasions that they were pleased you were joining them, that they had high hopes for you to "really make a difference," and that you were just the right person to do a really great job. Perhaps the exact words you heard are not what's written here, but there is little doubt that when a new principal comes to a school, people have high hopes that the newcomer will either accomplish the same things as his or her predecessor or make the kinds of changes that will immediately straighten up the mess left by the former principal. Variations on these two themes are possible, but people want the new principal to do all sorts of things, starting on the first day on the job.

As a beginner, you will have a natural tendency to try to please everyone, meet all expectations, and do a truly outstanding job at all times. But here's a secret: You can't do all the above. Furthermore, if you try to do everything with equal zeal and attention right away, you're likely to be less effective in your new job. Many researchers suggest that people proceed through clearly identified stages, or developmental phases, as they move into new roles.

Phase 1. This may be referred to as "coming on board." This period should normally last one or two years. It begins with a person first being named to a principalship. It ends at different times for different people, but generally it will end when a person feels comfortable enough with a new role that he or she is no longer concerned about losing the job for failing to do certain assigned tasks. People in this phase tend to be mostly concerned with their own survival. As a result, discussions about long-term goals and projects for a school or district are not particularly relevant. Furthermore, a principal in this phase is likely to think more about his or her personal needs than about any concerns related to the professional well-being of his or her staff.

Would you currently classify yourself as someone who is in this phase? Why?

_____

_____

_____

_____

_____

_____

_____

_____

Phase 2. After principals have developed some degree of comfort with the job and they are no longer experiencing any serious anxiety about trying to survive and simply do the job, they are likely to enter a second developmental phase. After about two years on the job, people should start to seek new ways of measuring effectiveness and success. This phase is classed as the "searching for success" time because principals at this point in their careers realize that they can do the job, but now they wish to do the job well. This phase is a progression beyond coming on board (Phase 1), but it is a time when principals are still likely to be more concerned with their own needs—or personal definitions of success—than they are with the broader needs of colleagues or the organization. However, there should be a definite shift from thinking only about survival as a reactive response to trying to move the school forward proactively. Again, no absolute timeline is established for this phase, but it is relatively brief for most people, lasting for only one or two years.

Is this a description of the phase of professional development in which you now find yourself? What implications for your long-term goals are based here?

_____

_____

_____

_____
_____
_____
_____
_____

Phase 3. This is a time of "looking outward." It is at this point that many principals start to question whether what they are doing is starting to have any positive effect on others. In some ways, it is very difficult to distinguish this stage from Phase 2, because during both phases, principals tend to focus on the impact of administrative behavior. The critical issue here, however, is that principals at this point are asking the questions, "Does what I do really have any effect on the teachers, staff, and most importantly, students?" and "Can I have a substantive impact on practices here so that we can improve the school?" One of the critical things to remember about this phase, if a principal enters it, is that the beginning of the phase may not happen until after three or four years of service. However, some principals may spend many years in their jobs without ever entering this phase. But in the case of good principals, it is also a phase that will never end.

Do you believe that you are at this phase, or are you still moving toward it? When do you plan on achieving the perspective of "looking outward?"

_____
_____
_____
_____
_____
_____
_____
_____

Phase 4. This stage in a principal's career, which may come sometime after about 10 years on the job, may be referred to as the "torch-passing" phase. This phase is the beginning of an interest in trying to find, recruit, and prepare other people to move into careers as educational leaders. Principals demonstrate this interest by (a) taking great pride in selecting specific individuals as assistants; (b) encouraging one or more of their teachers to think about future careers in school administration by taking courses at a local university; (c) taking on the duties of sponsorship and, to some extent, mentorship to draw new people into the profession; and (d) taking on their personal duties of developing the talents of others and improving the profession in general. Clearly, this phase is characterized by attention to the needs of others, the school or district, and the profession of the principalship. It is a significant departure from the first two phases, in which careers and interests are mostly directed inward. No defined period of time is associated with people moving into this career phase.

It may occur after five years as a principal, or after 15 or more years. In some cases, it may never be a part of an administrator's career phases.

Have you ever been the recipient of the care of a principal who was in the "torch-passing" phase? How has that had an impact on your career? Are you likely to try to adopt the same attitudes after you have gained more experience on the job?

_____

_____

_____

_____

_____

_____

_____

Phase 5. At this point in an individual's career, there is a distinct return to personal needs and agendas. Here, attention is focused on the process of "closing down a career." This might appear as getting ready for retirement or at least some sort of a shift into a career that is not the principalship. For instance, individuals get to a point where their interests are directed toward other positions such as superintendencies or other central office jobs. When a person reaches this point, he or she has more interest in other issues outside the daily responsibilities of the principalship.

Have you ever worked with a principal who was in the "closing out a career" phase? What behaviors were present in this administrator, and what impact did these behaviors have on the school in which you worked, or on your colleagues?

_____

_____

_____

_____

_____

_____

_____

A few summary observations are in order related to this list of different developmental phases. First, these five steps are not static or linear. In other words, people might move back and forth from one phase to another. For example, an individual who moves from one principalship to another might go from Phase 3 (looking outward) or even Phase 4 (torch passing) and return to Phase 2 (searching for success) when faced with the prospect of learning about new expectations, norms, and cultures of a different school and district. In fact, the only phases in this model that are found at relatively predictable points in an administrative career are Phase 1 (coming on board) at the beginning and Phase 5 (closing out a career) at the end. The second observation about the five phases is that not everyone proceeds through all steps. For example, some people never become interested in passing the torch (Phase 4) or even looking outward (Phase 3). They tend to remain interested in their own career needs, with little concern for colleagues. It may be unfortunate, but it is nevertheless a reality that people sometimes become so focused on their own situations that they forget about their professional relationships with others. It sometimes happens in personal relationships. Some people have also spent a large part of their careers in the coming on board phase (Phase 1); they never seem to learn or go beyond the limitations and perspectives of rookies. Suddenly, they shift from concerns, interests, and behaviors associated with newcomers to thinking about closing a career (Phase 5). These principals go through an entire career without getting out of the starting blocks. People probably don't intend to do this, but it can happen if one focuses too early and too quickly on simply serving as a principal without considering the associated responsibilities of providing leadership.

One final observation about the phases is that none of these steps is bounded by any strict time limits. For example, some people proceed quickly through the first three phases, often within the first two or three years of their professional lives. They spend the rest of their careers consciously serving as mentors to other practicing or aspiring educational administrators.

You can no doubt think of many examples of individual principals who were in one or another of these three phases. You may also wish to list some additional examples of what you have already encountered at one or more of the phases that I have identified.

_____

_____

_____

_____

_____

_____

_____

_____

WHAT'S THIS GOT TO DO WITH ME?

These phases may be of interest to those who are concerned with looking at and analyzing the long-term career paths of school administrators. But what relevance do they have for someone like you, who is either getting ready to step into a principalship for the first time or going through the first year or two on the job? After all, does it make any sense to think about serving as a mentor some day in the future while you are still trying to find a colleague to help you now?

Unless you look at how careers progress, you may be frustrated and limited as you start your life as a principal. Typically, individuals walk into a school system where colleague principals are distributed across all the phases, with one exception:

It is not unusual for a person to be the only principal who is coming on board (Phase 1) at a particular time. As a result, a person can get lost in an environment where everyone else is either thinking about retirement or focused exclusively on searching for success (Phase 2) as a personal concern. Any newly hired principal needs to find a mentor; however, some districts have no principals who are even remotely interested in torch passing (Phase 4). Finding a mentor will be discussed in greater detail in Chapter 14. When a district has no one to serve as a mentor, it may be necessary to seek support from an administrator in another school system.

In addition, knowing about this predictable progression might help you to think about your future life as an administrator. For example, it's important for you to recognize that for the next few years, you might spend a lot of time and energy thinking about personal needs. That's important. Numerous rookie principals have expressed anxiety and almost a sense of guilt over the fact that they were not accomplishing as much as they wanted to accomplish as quickly as they had hoped. They were not becoming effective instructional leaders as suggested in the research literature. Instead, they felt as if most of their time was being invested in personal concerns.

The first few years are likely to be the ones in which individuals establish their sense of identity and comfort in their roles. As one new principal once said, "I can't get too concerned about changing the world until I get my own house in order." It is perfectly understandable that you are probably not getting too involved with thoughts of torch passing just yet. On the other hand, you may be tempted to feel guilty about not getting involved in more than personal interests. After all, in many cases, new principals are alone as rookies in their school districts, and as a result it is not unusual for them to feel distant from colleagues and not completely committed to the goals and objectives of the larger system. As more than one beginning principal has noted over the years, "Before I become a great instructional leader, I just want to get through each day of my first year on the job."

Each new principal will have to establish his or her own realistic timeline that will permit movement from one phase to another. Some people will be able to move very quickly during the first few weeks of service from simply coming on board to Phase 2, in which they are seeking ways to improve the programs for students, teachers, parents, and the whole community. This might be due to a variety of reasons, such as the nature of their teaching staffs, the size of the district, the quality of their preservice preparation program (and internship experiences), whether they were an assistant principal in the past (and the nature of the interaction they had with their principals while in that role), whether they now have an assistant principal, whether they worked in this district as a teacher, and so on. Some people may need more than a year to go beyond initial culture shock and progress beyond the coming on board phase (Phase 1).

The important thing that any new principal needs to remember is that time spent as a rookie is valuable. Don't rush too quickly toward trying to learn a whole new system and change the world in one month simply because the research on school effectiveness says that principals must make an immediate difference. It simply is not going to happen overnight for everyone. And you should not get discouraged if you don't understand everything as quickly as you had hoped you might.

The key to effectiveness is neither going too fast nor dragging your feet waiting for the "perfect time" to foster change. Perhaps a very effective strategy to follow is the development of a realistic set of annual plans to guide your work. This is an organized way to initiate change while allowing you to look at your school objectively. This type of planning might begin during your second year as a principal, and it probably ought to continue throughout your career. On the following pages, I've provided an outline for this type of systematic planning.

DEVELOPING A PERSONAL TIMELINE FOR ACTION

A critical part of preparing a personal professional development portfolio and action plan involves not only stating *what* you want to do, but even more important, *when* you are going to do things. The last section of this chapter proposes that you develop a personal timeline that you will follow as you set out to meet certain professional goals during your first year on the job. Remember, you cannot accomplish everything at once, but you may never accomplish anything without a serious plan to determine which things are to happen first. Another helpful tip might be to make certain that you bounce these goals off a few people you trust. Seeking this type of feedback can be very useful to you in thinking about goals and priorities.

GOAL 1

The first goal I hope to accomplish in this first year as a principal is

_____

_____

_____

_____

_____

_____

_____

I hope to achieve this goal by doing the following:

_____

_____

_____

_____

_____

_____

_____

The latest date I expect to achieve this goal is

_____

_____

_____

_____

GOAL 2

The second goal that I hope to achieve in this first year as a principal is

_____

_____

_____

_____

_____

_____

_____

_____

I hope to achieve this goal by doing the following:

_____

_____

_____

_____

_____

_____

_____

_____

_____

The latest date I expect to achieve this goal is

_____

_____

_____

_____

GOAL 3

The third goal that I expect to accomplish during this first year as a principal is

_____

_____

_____

_____

_____

_____

_____

_____

I expect to achieve this goal by doing the following:

_____

_____

_____

_____

_____

_____

_____

_____

_____

The latest date that I hope to achieve this goal is

_____

_____

_____

_____

_____

_____

_____

This chapter concludes by providing a place above for you to write three goals, but this does not mean that as a first-year principal you shouldn't try to achieve more than three goals. At the same time, you should not try to do too many things at once. What is the right number of things for a rookie to try? That is a question only you can answer. How much is enough, and which things should be done first, is not something that this book can prescribe. Nor is it something that your superintendent, your school board, or central office can dictate. It is legitimate, of course, for superintendents to charge principals with goals that need to be addressed in all schools of the district. After all, you are part of a larger system. However, if a personal objective is simply to make certain that you do not do anything contrary to what your bosses tell you today, then you will do little more than follow the priorities as much as possible.

On the other hand, what you do, when you do it, and how you do it will always be matters that come from within you and your individual set of values and beliefs. Once again, the platform exercise described earlier is critical to your success. And sharing that platform with others—your staff as well as the superintendent—will do much to increase effective communication so that you meet the expectations of others and still focus on your personal objectives with equal commitment and zeal.

SUGGESTED READING

O'Mahoney, G., & Matthews, R. (2003). *Learning the role: Through the eyes of beginning principals.* Paper presented at the Annual Meeting of the American Educational Research Association, AERA.

Parkay, F., & Hall, G. (1991). *Becoming a principal: The challenges of beginning leadership.* Boston: Allyn & Bacon.

14

Building a Support System

Toni Spencer had just suffered through what was undoubtedly the single worst day of her first year as an elementary school principal. Before she had even left the house this morning, she got a call from Harriet Wilson, her secretary and virtual assistant principal, who said that she had a family emergency and would not be in today and perhaps the remainder of the week. When Toni arrived at school, she found Hank Gentry, her custodian, busily trying to scrub some fresh graffiti off one of the doors that led into the school from the playground. Next, while Toni was working with the substitute secretary (a woman who made it quite clear that she didn't like working in an elementary school because of "all the whining little kids") to orient her to the front office routine for the day, the phone rang almost incessantly. In less than five minutes, Toni received word that two teachers were going to be late and three more were ill and would not be in at all today. Substitutes would be needed. That was fine, except Toni knew that subs would be really hard to find this week. The neighboring Mountain City schools were in the midst of a lengthy teachers' strike, and their school board was bound and determined to keep the schools open by bringing in substitutes from every school district in the county and paying them a daily rate much higher than other systems. And that meant that Toni would not have a lot of luck in finding subs at the last minute. This was going to be one of those days when "creative class coverage" would take effect. Toni knew she would be in classrooms most of the morning.

Taking over classes from time to time was not something that Toni did not like. In fact, she looked forward to getting back in the trenches to work with the kids on occasion. But today, she knew that the president of her PTO would be visiting her school just before lunch to talk about the big spring fashion show. And Dr. Crawford, the district director of research and evaluation, was going to stop by to go over the state standardized achievement test results for her third and fifth graders. He was on a tight schedule and he insisted on releasing test results only during face-to-face sessions with each principal in the district. Today, Toni was on his list. She wasn't looking forward to the session because she had already heard from other elementary principals that the scores did not look good this year.

Despite all the things that were on her mind, Toni had the day pretty well under control by mid-morning. She felt as if this tough day was on the down side and that it would be over before it got any worse. She was just returning to her office from one of the fourth-grade classrooms where a substitute teacher couldn't find a class roster. Mrs. Turner, the substitute secretary, met her in the hall to tell her about a fifth-grade student who had just been brought down to the main office by the Phys Ed teacher for carrying a knife to class. She also heard that the fire marshal would be in today to pull a practice fire alarm, and the superintendent had called to say he was stopping by with a parent, but "he didn't want to discuss the issue over the phone." Toni was still in some degree of shock over the conversation she had a few minutes ago with a group of sixth-grade boys who told her they had seen a fifth grader passing out what they thought might be drugs on a vacant lot a few blocks from school earlier this morning.

The PTO president stopped by for what turned out to be anything but a productive conversation about the spring fashion luncheon. Instead, she used her time with the principal to lobby for changing her daughter from one kindergarten classroom to another because "other mothers" had told her that her daughter's teacher was very strict with the children. After convincing the mother that time would show that change was not really needed, Toni headed off for lunch, but this was another one of those days when "lunch" (two candy bars and a cup of instant coffee) didn't come until nearly 2:00. As soon as Toni was able to get to her office for a few minutes, she reflected on her discussion with the superintendent and the irate parent (who admitted after a few minutes that she really had not gotten all the facts from her son before she lost her temper and called the superintendent to complain about an alleged remark that Toni's teacher had made about the boy), and the fire drill (which went reasonably well but yielded a few minor violations that had to be corrected). She also handed out an in-school suspension penalty for the fifth-grade "knife" (actually, a can opener that probably wouldn't have even been challenged at the local airport) carrier, and put out about a dozen other small fires that had arisen during the day. Suddenly, her phone rang. An officer from the local police department was calling to alert her that she might be visited by a man claiming to be the father of one of her third graders. This same person—a known child molester—had appeared at other elementary schools in another suburb a few times over the past two weeks. If he did show up, Toni was advised to keep an eye on him, try to divert him from the children, and call the police immediately, all without doing anything to tip off the unwanted visitor before the police could arrive. The first thing that Toni did after getting off the phone was to visit each of her teachers and quietly explain the situation so that they would be aware of the potential problem. Just before 3:00, Dr. Crawford arrived with the test scores and indicated that Toni's third and fourth graders had passed, but they were quite close to failing the performance standards established for math. She was told that if this current school year's standards had been in place last spring, she would have had both grades failing. She knew that this information would appear on the front page of the *Tribune* either tomorrow or the next day.

Now it was nearly 5:00. Toni had already gotten word that her secretary would be out for the entire week, the substitute secretary didn't like how cold the office was, two of today's absent teachers would be out again tomorrow, and three more teachers were going to a district workshop on inclusion tomorrow. Toni faced the prospect of having at least five teachers out tomorrow, an unhappy secretary (who might not even report to work), and the consequences of a number of disciplinary decisions that she had had to make, including the in-school suspension. Angry parents were sure to be in her office tomorrow. But that would be after Toni got to work a bit late tomorrow because she would park down the street from the vacant lot where the drug dealing was supposedly taking place. She hadn't completely believed the story she heard today, but she couldn't afford to discount the tale entirely. She wanted to see things with her own eyes before she called the police. She was also quite sure that she would be one of the principals called by the newspaper to explain what happened on last year's math tests. Frankly, she wasn't surprised, but at this point, she didn't have any explanations to share with the press, either.

She was afraid that the imposter father might show up any time. In addition, Toni was worried about her own children—one of whom was a third grader at another school in the district. Her husband was out of town on a business trip, and her ninth-grade son was feeling depressed because he had been ignored by his basketball coach all season.

There are simply some days when you have to wonder why you do what you do!

Do the things that happened to Toni sound familiar? Perhaps you're lucky enough not to have a single day quite as bad as hers. Or maybe the day that Toni experienced was actually an easy day on your calendar. The point is that all principals, regardless of experience, level of school, size of school, type of school district, or any other variable that might be introduced, have very important, difficult, and demanding jobs. And the fact is that the job will likely become even more demanding, critical, and stressful in the future. As more states and school districts race toward the adoption of decentralized forms of school governance and administration, the spotlight will be directed even more on the principal's role in providing effective leadership. This first must be recognized along with the other types of demands, expectations, and pressures that are placed on educators in general, and principals in particular. Who could possibly imagine that elementary school principals (and principals in general) would some day be involved with planning escape routes and action plans in case students begin firing pistols and rifles on campus? And what about the need to work effectively with youngsters who walk into schools each day from homes where parents are child abusers, drug dealers, or other forms of felons and sociopaths? What do principals do when students arrive at their schools after spending the night on a floor or in a bathtub while listening to the sounds of gunshots in their neighborhoods, afraid that a stray bullet might crash through a window or door in their home?

The listing of problems faced by modern principals ends here. For one thing, continuing to list all the problems may cause you to question your decision about becoming a principal in the first place. Quite simply, the benefits of being a principal will likely far outweigh the problems and frustrations in the long run. Nevertheless, it is critical both for immediate survival and long-term success that you find some strategies to make certain that when the alligators are nipping at your ankles, you don't get swallowed up. Even Toni was able to come back and face another day!

This chapter offers a few strategies that have been identified by many very successful (and surviving) school principals who have learned how to cope with the numerous frustrations and pressures on the job. You may have already adopted some of these suggestions on your own, and in that case, you may be well beyond the advice offered here. Or you may be in that unfortunate state where the problems and crises have been coming along so rapidly in your life that you haven't had much time to look up from your desk and find any useful survival strategies. In that case, this chapter will be extremely important.

STRATEGY 1: FIND A MENTOR

The single most powerful thing a beginning principal (and even experienced principals) can do to enhance personal survival and effectiveness is to find at least one other experienced educational leader who can be available to share expertise related to doing the job more effectively and, perhaps even more important, help you to understand yourself and your personal transition into the principalship more completely. A mentor can also help significantly with the complex task of becoming effectively socialized into the profession of the principalship and also into the norms, culture, practices, and procedures of the school district in which you find your first job.

Do you already have at least one mentor who is helping you during this initial introduction to the principalship? (If so, who is it and what are some of the characteristics you have found in that person that make him or her particularly helpful to you as a mentor?)

_____

_____

_____

_____

_____

_____

_____

_____

Research on administrative mentors has found the following characteristics in individuals identified as effective mentors to aspiring and beginning school principals (compare these qualities with ones on the list you have prepared above).

1. Mentors are experienced administrators who are regarded by peers and others as effective.

2. Mentors demonstrate qualities of effective leaders, such as

   - good communications skills,
   - intelligence,
   - a clear vision of what could be,
   - positive interpersonal skills and sensitivity.

3. Mentors ask the right questions; they do not simply provide the right answers.

4. Mentors accept others' ways of doing things; they do not want everyone else to do it their way.

5. Mentors desire other people to go beyond their present levels of performance.

6. Mentors model principles of continuous learning and reflection.

7. Mentors exhibit awareness of the practical and social realities of life in at least one school system.

You may have noticed the absence of some other characteristics that a lot of people have often assumed to be desirable for mentors. For example, many people assume that the most effective mentors are those with many years of experience as principals, as if survival on the job automatically results in wisdom and insight. Some individuals may spend 20 years as principals, but unfortunately, they have done the same things for 20 years in a row! Consequently, they haven't grown, and they haven't learned from their past experiences. What are you likely to gain from working with people like this?

People also assume that men must mentor men, and only women can mentor women. Although people often express a preference for same-gender mentoring relationships (and for some reason these are easier to carry out), no research shows conclusively that men cannot be effective mentors to women (or vice versa). This is a comforting finding, particularly in the world of high school administration in which relatively few experienced female high school principals can be found to mentor beginning female colleagues.

People also incorrectly assume that only older individuals can serve effectively as mentors to younger administrators. Perhaps this image comes from the traditional view that the only thing that a mentor does is fill the protégé up with a lot of tricks of the trade and lessons from the past. That is a very limited view of mentoring and one that has the potential of being more harmful than helpful to your career. The reason is that in many cases, new principals have been hired precisely because of the desire to get some new blood in the school system. There has been too long a history of doing the same things in the same way. Mentors who see themselves only as people to help you do your job in an easier way may be inadvertently limiting your potential success by telling you "how we've always done it around here."

Now that you have considered these additional issues regarding effective mentoring relationships, who are some individuals who may be effective mentors for you as a beginning principal? (These may not be the same people you thought of at the beginning of this chapter.)

_____

_____

_____

_____

_____

_____

_____

Be aware that you may be assigned a mentor by your employing school district. In recent years, districts are paying attention to the needs of beginners, either because there is a recognition that this is good practice, or because a number of states now require mentors to be assigned to educators who are in their first year of service. In many cases, well-intentioned districts simply select senior administrators (i.e., those with the greatest number of years of experience) or retired local principals to mentor newcomers. There is no doubt that you can learn from these individuals. But you might need to go beyond the matches that are made at the central office and seek your own mentor as well. It never hurts to have more than one person helping you.

STRATEGY 2: DEVELOP NETWORKS

Another strategy to help you in the first years of the principalship is to develop networks with other administrators. These relationships can take several different forms. For example, if you are one of several rookie principals in a district, county, or some other identifiable region, you may wish to get in contact with these other inexperienced administrators to form some kind of mutual support group. You might decide to get together once a month for a social gathering during which you can share some of your war stories (or horror stories) about your life as a beginner. You will no doubt be surprised to learn that many of the "mistakes" that you believe you have made are ones made by a good many of your beginning colleagues (and more experienced colleagues as well).

Do you know of other beginning principals in your area with whom you might be able to form a mutual support network?

_____

_____

_____

_____

_____

_____

_____

_____

Networks have also been formed among women principals. Only a few years ago this was a rarity. Now women administrator leagues and networks have appeared all over the country, generally based on the assumption that because school administration has traditionally been viewed as a "man's game," it is critical to develop mutually supportive arrangements among those who want a share of the "game." The same logic has been shared in the establishment of networks for representatives of ethnic and racial minority groups serving as school leaders.

The formation of networks is an important form of support that may assist you in the earliest stages of your career, with an important exception. In some cases, the primary goal of a network apparently has been only to maintain itself, not necessarily to provide support to individual participants. It is likely that as one matures in a professional role, it will be less important to maintain membership in a mutual support arrangement, whether the arrangement is classified as mentoring or a network. In those cases, it is important that you feel free to determine your own continuing membership. A relationship of any kind is no longer healthy when participants feel as if they are forced to continue to stay involved.

Are you currently already affiliated with one or more professional development networks? What are some of the benefits that you derive from this association with others?

_____

_____

_____

_____

_____

_____

_____

_____

STRATEGY 3: PARTICIPATE IN PROFESSIONAL ASSOCIATIONS

As you begin a new career, you will receive invitations for membership in professional associations that provide many opportunities for you to stay abreast of current educational issues and to become politically involved. Although these organizations require some dedication of your time and financial resources, you should consider membership as a commitment to the improvement of not only your profession but also your own career.

Whether it is the National Association of Elementary School Principals (NAESP), the National Association of Secondary School Principals (NASSP), the National Middle Schools Association (NMSA), or the state and local affiliates of these nationwide organizations, belonging to one or more appropriate professional associations has some clear benefits. For example, you receive publications such as the NASSP *Bulletin* or the NAESP *Principal* magazines several times each year. These and many other fine newsletters and reports provided by the associations will help you to remain in contact with important research, trends, and issues that face principals all over the United States. Most state affiliates also offer periodic publications to keep you informed about matters of local interest to you and your colleagues.

Membership in professional associations also usually provides you with some sort of professional liability insurance coverage. Both NASSP and NAESP and their local affiliates also offer legal services hotlines that enable members to get feedback from attorneys and experienced administrators as they go about their daily work. Finally, membership in professional associations allows you to attend workshops, seminars, conferences, and conventions that help you maintain important professional, social, and political contact with other principals across your state and around the United States.

Perhaps the single most important value to be gained from members in relevant professional associations, however, has little to do with publications, legal services, liability insurance, or attendance at conventions. Simply stated, when you become involved in a national association of professional school administrators, you develop a sense of belonging and involvement with your profession. By reading publications of your associations, attending meetings, and serving on committees, task forces, or other kinds of activities, you have a chance to hear or read about the world of administration as experienced by your colleagues in other settings. Often, the job of principal feels like a lonely one because it seems that the problems and issues that you encounter are of such magnitude that no one else has ever faced these concerns. Working with colleagues from other school systems (and perhaps from other states, on occasion) is a quick way to establish that you are not alone. Others are walking in your shoes.

Professional association memberships cost money, and that is a resource most principals do not have as a surplus, particularly in the first few years of their careers. Often, your first principalship comes soon after you have completed (and paid for) graduate courses at a university. You may have also recently had to pay to relocate to a new community. In some cases, new principals report receiving less pay than they were earning as classroom teachers. Nevertheless, membership in appropriate state, local, and national associations is a worthwhile investment that can assist you in your daily life as a professional administrator.

What professional associations do you belong to, and what professional conferences or seminars do you plan to attend next year? What publications for principals do you try to read on a regular basis?

_____

_____

_____

_____

_____

_____

_____

_____

If you are not currently involved with one or more professional associations, do you plan to join any group in the foreseeable future? Why or why not?

_____

_____

_____

_____

_____

_____

_____

STRATEGY 4: MAINTAIN PERSONAL AND FAMILY SUPPORT

The fourth and final form of support may be the most obvious one, but it is often overlooked as people embark upon new careers. Often, the most powerful way to help newcomers to a field is found in one's natural, immediate environment. As you begin your career as an administrator, it is likely that your world will be filled with so many new responsibilities, people, and activities that you will become overwhelmed with many competing demands and interests. Suddenly, things and events that were important to you only a few months ago seem distant and less important as you work hard to develop a new professional identity and self-image. Although that is understandable, it is critical to keep a personal focus on what is truly important in your life. Demands of a professional nature are important; the roots and foundation in your personal family life are even more important and will be with you beyond your career as the principal of a school.

The first recommendation, then, is to make certain that, whenever possible, you do whatever is needed and reasonable to retain some sense of normality in your personal life. Do not ignore family and friends. If you are a high school principal with numerous night and weekend duties, don't forget your own son's piano recital, or your daughter's basketball tournament. Remember that the annual family trek to the shore was a big part of your life when you were a fourth-grade teacher; it is still important now that you are an elementary school principal. Don't forget to return phone calls to personal friends who knew you back in the old days, before you were such an important person. In short, keep your compass and perspective; don't forget who or what is really important to you. And remember that you can be a very effective and successful leader if you take a night off to do nothing more critical than watch a sappy old move on DVD.

What are some things that you have done to retain contact with important friends and family members?

_____

_____

_____

_____

_____

_____

_____

_____

The second recommendation is related to your need to maintain your health. Critically ill principals are not very effective. Do not neglect matters of health, personal fitness, and well-being. This is important with respect to matters of physical wellness and also emotional, intellectual, and even spiritual well-being. Go to the doctor when you are sick and for regular examinations. Exercise, eat right (and don't fall into the "principal-as-martyr syndrome" that seemingly rewards people for never eating lunch, skipping breakfast, and drinking coffee all day), and take care of your body. Get out of your office, forget about your work every once in a while, read a good suspense novel, attend a movie or concert, or do any of a thousand things that will remind you that you have a personal life and that you need to get out of your formal role as an educational leader on occasion. (This reminder may be a difficult one for you. Educators are notorious for their tendency to eat, drink, and sleep "school stuff" and talk shop all the time.)

What are some of the ways in which you address your health and wellness needs now?

_____

_____

_____

_____

_____

_____

_____

With regard to intellectual well-being, do something that challenges your mental capacity. Some school principals regularly take university courses or participate in study groups that have nothing to do with the field of education as a way to keep their minds sharp; they enroll in language courses or other programs that seemingly avoid educational topics as a way to keep contact with their spiritual core. And with regard to spiritual well-being, if you have been involved with religious activities throughout your life, is there any reason to stop this involvement simply because you have the title of "principal" over your door?

In what ways do you address your personal needs for emotional, intellectual, and spiritual health?

_____

_____

_____

_____

_____

_____

_____

It is not possible to prescribe all the things you might do to ensure that you maintain a proper balance in your priorities as a beginning principal. I'm not suggesting that the only route to happiness and success will be to maintain a perfect family life. After all, principals have situations in their personal lives during which the traditional pattern of home and happiness might be interrupted or changed. And those situations might have nothing to do with their effectiveness as a principal or their personal well-being. At times, it will be impossible to get to the gym, play a round of golf, or attend an opera, even though these activities might well be worthwhile. The critical message here is that it is not only a good idea, but in some ways a critical responsibility for principals to think of their own needs above other issues. In this regard, you may wish to think about the insightful comment often made by Roland Barth, founder of the Harvard Principals' Center and frequent contributor to the literature on leadership and the professional development of school principals. Barth has often observed that when you get on an airplane, the flight attendants state that in an emergency that causes the cabin to lose pressurization, air masks will fall from the compartments in the ceiling. They tell you to put your own mask on first before you try to help others around you. Barth uses this to illustrate that it is important for principals to take care of their own needs first, lest they no longer be able to do the job of helping others when needed.

DEVELOPING A PLAN OF ACTION

This chapter concludes by asking you to plan a systematic way of putting into effect many of the support mechanisms identified here. It is absolutely important to select some clear ways in which you might reasonably expect to enjoy greater success in your job. By taking the time to write out some of the sources of support you may find for yourself, you will become committed to these various approaches and activities.

Strategy 1: Find a Mentor

Who are some individuals who could serve in a mentoring capacity to you as you move into the principalship?

_____
_____
_____
_____
_____
_____
_____
_____

What are some of the specific concerns associated with your work as a principal that you believe might be addressed through a mentoring relationship?

_____
_____
_____
_____
_____
_____

_____

_____

Strategy 2: Develop Networks

Do you currently have any networks developed with other school principals?

_____
_____
_____
_____
_____
_____
_____
_____

In what specific ways might a network assist you in dealing with concerns and issues that you are now facing as a beginning principal?

_____
_____
_____
_____
_____
_____
_____
_____

Strategy 3: Participate in Professional Associations

Do you currently belong to any state, local, or national associations for school administrators? Which one(s)?

_____
_____
_____
_____
_____
_____

What are some activities of your association in which you participate? What personal or professional goals do you hope to achieve through these forms of participation?

_____

_____

_____

_____

_____

_____

_____

Strategy 4: Maintain Personal and Family Support

List some of the ways you intend to spend more time with your family and friends, engage in leisure activities, or simply take care of yourself during the next several months.

_____

_____

_____

_____

_____

_____

_____

What are some of the personal and professional benefits you hope to achieve?

_____

_____

_____

_____

_____

_____

_____

15

Some Concluding Thoughts

Each of the previous chapters has featured at least one case study or scenario presented to illustrate some of the key issues that were raised in the chapters. These have all been based on actual issues shared with me by many first- and second-year principals with whom I have had the pleasure of working over the years. I hope that these materials have been helpful to you as you go about your personal "voyage of beginning the principalship." This last chapter includes material not found in the first two editions of this book. Here, the intention is not to illustrate a single concept such as learning how to analyze the culture of your school, assess your personal leadership skills, or address the expectations and mandates for more accountable practice in your school.

Instead, I provide a number of random insights and tips that I have picked up from some excellent educators over the past several years. Each item represents a unique perspective related to your world as a school leader, and I trust that much of what is shared here will assist you not only in surviving as a beginning principal, but more importantly, thriving as an educational leader. There are no pseudonyms used in this chapter. Rather, the names have not been changed so that credit may be given to a great group of colleagues and educators.

NOT JUST A JOB

Jim Kelch is currently the assistant superintendent for personnel services in his school district. Prior to that, he was a high school principal and assistant principal in two very large high schools in a neighboring school district. While principal, his schools won numerous awards for excellence. One high school was designated as a National Blue Ribbon School, and other schools in which he worked were successful in terms of college placements and performance on statewide measures of achievement. Jim was recognized as the "Principal of the Year" in his region of the state, and the state principals' association designated him as a member of a select group of leaders serving as mentor principals to beginning colleagues across the state.

Spending a few minutes with Jim quickly reveals that the awards and achievements were accompanied by many other moments as a principal that were extremely challenging and, at times, downright frustrating. He admits that there were many times when the awesome responsibility and demands associated with leading schools with nearly 3,000 students led him to a sense of despair. Yet he persisted in his efforts to make certain that his students learned, his teachers taught, and that the community was proud of their local high schools.

> "Despite your accomplishments, it strikes me that you are painting a rather negative image of what it means to take the job of high school principal, Jim," I noted in a recent conversation. "In fact, one might ask, 'Who in their right mind would want your job?'"

> "To be honest, there have been a number of times when I really wondered if I was in my right mind doing the kinds of things that I had to do each day as a principal," my friend responded. "But I have always tried to keep in my mind a single fact. You simply cannot take on the principalship and view it as a job. It's not a job like any other role that you might select. If you think it's a job, you might have to conclude that it's a lousy job. The hours are long, the stress is high, the pay is low when you think of the long hours, and you rarely get credit when things go right. But you always are criticized when things go wrong!"

> "So, let me repeat my question. Who in their right mind would take the job of principal?"

> "The principalship is not a job. Simply stated, you have to view it as a special kind of calling. You will never be paid enough, nor get the kind of recognition that you might get as an executive in private business. You won't get many awards named in your honor. But you will get a lot of satisfaction if you hear the calling and respond to it. I'm not trying to make it sound like a religious event. But I firmly believe that if you can find yourself looking beyond the daily frustrations and seeing the really good things that can happen for kids and families, it makes the problems seem small. That's why to this day I miss the principalship."

Jim Kelch is truly a school leader who puts students at the center of his efforts. Not long ago, he exemplified this value when he stood between a police sharpshooter and a disturbed student who held a shotgun to his head while threatening to shoot other students and himself. By serving as a human shield so that he could talk the young man into giving up his plan, he clearly modeled the fact that there is indeed much more to being a principal than simply running a school.

KEEP YOUR SENSE OF HUMOR

"If you took to heart all the things that seem like tragedies each day in a school, you'd leave the principalship in a heartbeat," observed Debbie Livingston, another principal recently transplanted from a school campus to a central office position. "In the middle schools where I served as principal, we had a lot of children with serious problems. They were poor; they came from broken homes. We had problems with gangs. Lots of things were not pleasant. I'd have some very tough conversations in my office on some days, with students and also their parents. We had days when police came in to look for students, and I never thought I'd be able to get out of meetings."

"So you must be really ecstatic about getting out of the principal's office to a job in the central office."

"Don't get me wrong. I like what I'm doing now, and I have great colleagues. I believe that I'm involved with work that has payoffs for the whole district. But I miss the principalship."

I pointed to the number of problems that she had listed earlier in our conversation and wondered why anyone would miss the problems.

"I don't miss the problems. I miss the ability to solve them. And I miss the fun of being a principal. I enjoyed my work. I loved the kids, and I really enjoyed the friendships and spirit that you feel when working with a staff. I had great assistants in my different schools. I liked starting the day with sharing jokes with the office staff. There is a life that you feel in the principalship because you are part of a lively organization."

"So you really looked forward to getting back to your office every day?"

"Not my office. I always felt a bit like being a prisoner in that room every day. I miss the school. I loved seeing the small things that go on, the interactions teachers have with students, the wit of the kids, the happiness of the whole place. And it was always a place where my personal concerns always felt small compared to the real issues facing students, teachers, parents, staff members. If I got down with every frustration that I experienced each day, I would go nuts. You have to have the ability to laugh and enjoy the good things. You have to have a sense of humor and see the good in everything."

On the many occasions when I had the joy of walking around the school with her, Debbie Livingston sincerely walked her talk. Every face smiled at the happy leader who seemed to float through her building.

HOW FAR ARE YOU WILLING TO GO?

Gilbert Villagrana was born in Mexico and came to the United States when he was a teenager. Like so many immigrants from his country, he looked forward to a new life filled with opportunities not only for himself, but for his wife and children. His door opened when he landed a job in one school district. He served as a school janitor for a few years in that system, then moved on to a larger district where he was a head custodian in several different schools during the past 20 years.

When Gilbert spoke in my class a few years back, he began his presentation by asking the audience for patience since his English "wasn't too good." And he also stated that he would not be talking from the perspective of a professional educator. At the conclusion of his class presentation, one graduate student raised her hand and stated, "Mr. Villagrana, thank you for your insights. But you lied to us when you started. You communicated exceptionally well; your ability to express your ideas went well beyond any limitations in a particular language. And as far as not being a professional educator, you have greater insights into the needs of children and schools than many of us who have advanced degrees and years of experience in classrooms."

Gilbert merited these comments by noting that, as far as he was concerned, serving as a school custodian has been a way to allow him to serve everyone in his school. "I have served as a kind of counselor to kids who would never open up to teachers; I was Santa Claus at one school for a whole neighborhood filled with poor kids who would never have a chance to get to the fancy department stores at Christmas time; I've fixed broken shoes for teachers during the school day; I stayed up all night when police thought that we had a bomb planted in our school and they needed someone to open the doors and show them the possible hiding places; and I even substituted for a basketball coach who couldn't make it to the game on time one night." When I asked him if this was what other custodians would do, he said emphatically that "there are many people out there who are willing to go the extra mile for the students. But it's always a simple choice of making a decision when you ask yourself, 'How far are you willing to go?'"

As I have gotten to know and respect this remarkable person over the years, I realize that he could be one of the many "invisible heroes" that work in our schools each day. The fact is that there are many others like Gilbert. When you find them, cherish them.

MAKE YOUR SCHOOL YOUR FAMILY

One of the questions that consistently arises from both beginners to educational administration and graduate students who are contemplating future careers in administration concerns the problem with maintaining a personal life given the heavy time demands of the principalship. Nick Cobos, another colleague who left public education after 30 years, 20 of which were in administrative positions in middle schools and high schools, and now serves as a private school principal, is another individual whose dedication to schools and students is exemplary. He is married and has three children, two of whom recently graduated as commissioned officers from the U.S. Military Academy at West Point, and one who is about to enter law school after completing her undergraduate studies in three years. His wife is also an educator.

When asked how he was able to maintain a happy home life as he spent many hours on the job as a secondary school teacher, Nick's response was one that might help you as you consider the pressures of doing your job and being at home.

"First of all, I made certain that my kids always went to the high schools in which I served as principal. That took some effort in each case. For all three,

I had to make special arrangements with my employing district since I actually lived in a different school district than where my schools were located. It took some requests for waivers, but it was well worth it to be able to share my school life with my kids each day. Some people say that kids of principals hate going to the school where he or she works. I really believe my three really enjoyed it, but they never tried playing the 'But my dad is your boss' game with any teachers. I never would put up with that. My wife joined our 'extended family' at school as well. When I had to work at football games in the fall or basketball games during the winter, she'd come to school with us and become one of the cheering spectators."

Indeed, few football games did not see Mr. and Mrs. Cobos standing side-by-side on the sidelines.

"The point is, I cared for all my students and their families as I cared for my own. I loved the schools and the students wherever I worked. My own family, of course, always comes first, but I was always able to keep everything together. It worked for us."

The fact is that if you can remember that your "job" is truly a "calling," and if you keep your sense of focus and humor, and if you are willing to go far with your commitment, you can always keep your eyes on the target of devoting yourself to all things that are important to you. Creating a true community for learning is very much like being the head of your own family.

KEEP YOUR EYE ON THE TARGET

The last person I wanted to share with you as you ponder the awesome nature of your job as a school principal is a great friend who works with me now at the University of Texas at El Paso. She is Sandra Hurley, now a university administrator who previously served as a teacher of reading education and also as a supervisor and administrator in a local school district. Her advice to me in moments of my frustration has always been a consistent, simple statement: "Never take your eyes off the real target—the kids. Never forget the reason why we are all here. We opted for jobs in this business because we want good things to happen for our students." It is always a great relief when I have the chance to hear Sandra share those insights. It brings me (and hopefully you as well) quickly back to recognizing the most important aspects of our work.

LAST WORDS

The enjoyable part of writing this last chapter is not the fact that I could write a few kind words about five great educators who can serve as examples of all that is good about leadership in schools. The fact is, I have been able to call hundreds of great leadership role models friends over the years, and they work in huge city school districts like Chicago and also in very small towns in Colorado, Wisconsin, and Ohio. They are experienced principals who have moved on to other positions in education, and also relatively inexperienced leaders who are in the first years of their first administrative assignments. The key question to be asked is simply, "If you had a chance to revisit your decision, would you choose the job you have now, as a principal, again?" The answer, fortunately for all of us, is always the same: "Yes!"

Being a principal is a lot of hard work. And because it is tough work, it is a place where individual disappointment can be quite high. Remember one thing, however. Not many people go into any career with an expectation that they will ever do anything less than a "perfect" job. But as you consider how good you want to be and how much you want to be an effective school leader, remember the game of golf. In its entire history, there have been many fantastic and talented golfers, to be sure. But in the millions of games of golf played over the years, I know of no golfer—from Babe Zacharias to Arnold Palmer to Nancy Lopez to Jack Nicklaus to Annika Sorenstam to Tiger Woods—who has ever had a perfect game. That means no one has ever gotten a score of 18 on 18 holes of golf. And in all probability, there never will be anyone who is "perfect." By the same token, there are many very talented and effective principals. But each one has had bad days; made mistakes; and gotten frustrated with parents, central office administrators, and indeed, students themselves.

So the final note is that while you may never be perfect, keep hitting the balls off the tee as hard as you can, and putt with effectiveness and certainty that you will do as good a job as possible.

Good luck, and have a great time "beginning the principalship."

Appendix

Beginning Principals' Administrative Skills Assessment Instrument

PERFORMANCE DOMAINS ASSESSMENT

DIRECTIONS: *For each of the following items, circle the number (from 1 to 7) that represents your assessment of your ability related to that particular skill. (1 = VERY WEAK and 7 = VERY STRONG)*

LEADERSHIP: Providing purpose and direction for individuals   1 2 3 4 5 6 7
and groups; shaping school culture and values; facilitating the development
of a shared strategic vision for the school; formulating goals and
planning change efforts with staff; setting priorities for one's school
in the context of community and district priorities and student
and staff needs.

INFORMATION COLLECTION: Gathering data, facts, and impressions   1 2 3 4 5 6 7
from a variety of sources about students, parents, staff members,
administrators, and community members; seeking knowledge
about policies, rules, laws, precedents, or practices; managing the data
flow; classifying and organizing information for use in decision
making and monitoring.

PROBLEM ANALYSIS: Identifying the important elements of a problem   1 2 3 4 5 6 7
situation by analyzing relevant information; framing problems; identifying
possible causes; seeking additional needed information; framing and
reframing possible solutions; exhibiting conceptual flexibility; assisting
others to form reasoned opinions about problems and issues.

JUDGMENT: Reaching logical conclusions and making high quality,   1 2 3 4 5 6 7
timely decisions based on the best available information; exhibiting
tactical adaptability; giving priority to significant issues.

ORGANIZATIONAL OVERSIGHT: Planning and scheduling one's own   1 2 3 4 5 6 7
and others' work so that resources are used appropriately and short- and
long-term priorities are met; scheduling flows of activities; establishing
procedures to regulate activities; monitoring projects to meet deadlines;
empowering the process in appropriate places.

IMPLEMENTATION: Making things happen; putting programs and change   1 2 3 4 5 6 7
efforts into action; facilitating coordination and collaboration of tasks;
establishing project checkpoints and monitoring progress; providing
"mid-course" corrections when actual outcomes start to diverge from
intended outcomes or when conditions require adaptation; supporting those
responsible for carrying out projects and plans.

DELEGATION: Assigning tasks, projects, and responsibilities   1 2 3 4 5 6 7
together with clear authority to accomplish them in a timely and
acceptable manner; utilizing subordinates effectively; following up on
delegated activities.

INSTRUCTION AND THE LEARNING ENVIRONMENT: Creating a school   1 2 3 4 5 6 7
culture for learning; envisioning and enabling with others instructional and
auxiliary programs for the improvement of teaching and learning; recognizing
the developmental needs of students; ensuring appropriate instructional
methods; designing positive learning experiences in cognition and

achievement; mobilizing the participation of appropriate people or groups to develop these programs and to establish a positive learning environment.

CURRICULUM DESIGN: Understanding major curriculum design models; interpreting school district curricula; initiating needs analyses; planning and implementing with staff a framework for instruction; aligning curriculum with anticipated outcomes; monitoring social and technological developments as they affect curriculum; adjusting content as needs and conditions change.

1 2 3 4 5 6 7

STUDENT GUIDANCE: Understanding and accommodating student growth and development; providing for student guidance, counseling, and auxiliary services; utilizing and coordinating community organizations; responding to family needs; enlisting the participation of appropriate people and groups to design and conduct these programs and to connect schooling with plans for adult life; planning for a comprehensive program of student activities.

1 2 3 4 5 6 7

STAFF DEVELOPMENT: Working with faculty and staff to identify professional needs; planning, organizing, and facilitating programs that improve faculty and staff effectiveness and are consistent with institutional goals and needs; supervising individuals or groups; providing feedback on performance; arranging for remedial assistance; engaging faculty and others to plan and participate in recruitment and development activities; and initiating self-development.

1 2 3 4 5 6 7

MEASUREMENT AND EVALUATION: Determining what diagnostic information is needed about students, staff, and the school environment; examining the extent to which outcomes meet or exceed previously defined standards, goals, or priorities for individuals or groups; drawing inferences for program revisions; interpreting measurements or evaluation for others; relating programs to desired outcomes; developing equivalent measures of competence; designing accountability mechanisms.

1 2 3 4 5 6 7

RESOURCE ALLOCATION: Procuring, apportioning, monitoring, accounting for, and evaluating fiscal, human, material, and time resources to reach outcomes that reflect the needs and goals of the school site; planning and developing the budget process with appropriate staff.

1 2 3 4 5 6 7

MOTIVATING OTHERS: Creating conditions that enhance the staff's desire and willingness to focus energy on achieving educational excellence; planning and encouraging participation; facilitating teamwork and collegiality; treating staff as professionals; providing intellectual stimulation; supporting innovation; recognizing and rewarding effective performance; providing feedback, coaching, and guidance; providing needed resources; serving as a role model.

1 2 3 4 5 6 7

INTERPERSONAL SENSITIVITY: Perceiving the needs and concerns of others; dealing tactfully with others in emotionally stressful situations or in conflict; managing conflict; obtaining feedback; recognizing multicultural differences; relating to people of varying backgrounds.

1 2 3 4 5 6 7

ORAL AND NONVERBAL EXPRESSION: Making oral presentations that are clear and easy to understand; clarifying and restating questions; responding, reviewing, and summarizing for groups; utilizing appropriate communication aids; being aware of cultural and gender-based norms; adapting for audiences.

1 2 3 4 5 6 7

WRITTEN EXPRESSION: Expressing ideas clearly in writing; writing appropriately for different audiences such as students, teachers, and parents; preparing brief memoranda, letters, reports, and other job-specific documents.

1 2 3 4 5 6 7

PHILOSOPHICAL AND CULTURAL VALUES: Acting with a reasoned understanding of the role of education in a democratic society and in accordance with accepted ethical standards; recognizing philosophical influences in education; reflecting an understanding of American culture, including current social and economic issues related to education.

1 2 3 4 5 6 7

LEGAL AND REGULATORY APPLICATIONS: Acting in accordance with federal and state constitutional provisions, statutory standards, and regulatory applications; working within local rules, procedures, and directives; recognizing standards of care involving civil and criminal liability for negligence and intentional torts; and administering contracts and financial accounts.

1 2 3 4 5 6 7

POLICY AND POLITICAL INFLUENCES: Understanding schools as political systems; identifying relationships between public policy and education; recognizing policy issues; examining and affecting policies individually and through professional and public groups; relating policy initiatives to the welfare of students; addressing ethical issues.

1 2 3 4 5 6 7

PUBLIC RELATIONS: Developing common perceptions about school issues; interacting with internal and external publics; understanding and responding skillfully to the electronic and print news media; initiating and reporting news through appropriate channels; managing school reputations; enlisting public participation and support; recognizing and providing for various markets.

1 2 3 4 5 6 7

ASSESSMENT OF PERFORMANCE OF NATIONAL STANDARDS

DIRECTIONS: *For each item, please circle the number (from 1 to 7) that corresponds to your assessment of your strengths related to a particular Performance Competency. (1 = VERY WEAK and 7 = VERY STRONG)*

> *STANDARD ONE: The effective principal maximizes student learning by working with staff to translate knowledge of learning theory and human development and relevant school data into successful curricular programs, instructional practices, and assessment strategies.*

PERFORMANCE COMPETENCIES:

1. Setting, communicating, and monitoring high expectations for faculty and staff.

1 2 3 4 5 6 7

2. Nurturing the development of a shared school vision and mission.

1 2 3 4 5 6 7

3. Demonstrating a knowledge of learning theory.

1 2 3 4 5 6 7

4. Demonstrating sensitivity toward developmental levels.　　1　2　3　4　5　6　7

5. Learning how students are doing.　　1　2　3　4　5　6　7

6. Promoting the active involvement of all students.　　1　2　3　4　5　6　7

7. Encouraging risk taking and being receptive to change.　　1　2　3　4　5　6　7

8. Promoting divergent thinking.　　1　2　3　4　5　6　7

9. Promoting an attitude of inquiry.　　1　2　3　4　5　6　7

10. Encouraging teachers to maintain their visions.　　1　2　3　4　5　6　7

11. Organizing and conducting staff development.　　1　2　3　4　5　6　7

12. Modeling lifelong learning.　　1　2　3　4　5　6　7

13. Actively participating in professional development and as a teacher.　　1　2　3　4　5　6　7

14. Acting as a resource for teachers.　　1　2　3　4　5　6　7

15. Providing teachers with research that helps shape and improve.　　1　2　3　4　5　6　7

16. Acknowledging and rewarding continuous development of teachers.　　1　2　3　4　5　6　7

17. Implementing effective assessment procedures.　　1　2　3　4　5　6　7

18. Identifying and using data relevant to the school.　　1　2　3　4　5　6　7

19. Conveying appropriate data in a useful fashion and timely manner.　　1　2　3　4　5　6　7

20. Explaining and using student assessment data to develop the school plan and help staff shape the instructional and curricular program.　　1　2　3　4　5　6　7

21. Encouraging the use of varied approaches to assessment.　　1　2　3　4　5　6　7

22. Organizing the staff to facilitate learning.　　1　2　3　4　5　6　7

23. Facilitating development of an instructional program appropriate to the needs and developmental levels of students.　　1　2　3　4　5　6　7

24. Monitoring the implementation of instructional practices.　　1　2　3　4　5　6　7

25. Promoting the development of a safe, orderly climate for learning.　　1　2　3　4　5　6　7

26. Securing resources and materials to implement the instructional program.　　1　2　3　4　5　6　7

27. Collecting and analyzing data on teacher performance on a regular basis.　　1　2　3　4　5　6　7

28. Using staff evaluation information for the improvement of instruction.　　1　2　3　4　5　6　7

29. Providing meaningful feedback to teachers.   1 2 3 4 5 6 7

30. Employing technology to enhance the instructional program.   1 2 3 4 5 6 7

STANDARD TWO: The effective principal applies human relations and interpersonal skills to foster a climate of continuous learning and improvement.

PERFORMANCE COMPETENCIES:

31. Recognizing and being sensitive to individual differences.   1 2 3 4 5 6 7

32. Demonstrating an interest in others.   1 2 3 4 5 6 7

33. Being considerate of others.   1 2 3 4 5 6 7

34. Establishing credibility.   1 2 3 4 5 6 7

35. Maintaining accessibility and credibility.   1 2 3 4 5 6 7

36. Creating healthy dissatisfaction with the status quo.   1 2 3 4 5 6 7

37. Inviting risk taking.   1 2 3 4 5 6 7

38. Promoting enthusiasm.   1 2 3 4 5 6 7

39. Creating a win-win environment.   1 2 3 4 5 6 7

40. Monitoring staff morale.   1 2 3 4 5 6 7

41. Providing support.   1 2 3 4 5 6 7

42. Recognizing accomplishments.   1 2 3 4 5 6 7

43. Planning and organizing to involve community, parents, teachers, and students in decisions.   1 2 3 4 5 6 7

44. Seeking opportunities to share power—empowering others.   1 2 3 4 5 6 7

45. Actively involving others in the decision-making process.   1 2 3 4 5 6 7

46. Modeling the facilitator role in shared decision making.   1 2 3 4 5 6 7

47. Ensuring that there is equitable access to the decision-making process.   1 2 3 4 5 6 7

48. Fostering open communication.   1 2 3 4 5 6 7

49. Using effective organizational skills.   1 2 3 4 5 6 7

50. Modeling team building.   1 2 3 4 5 6 7

51. Using effective oral and written communication.   1 2 3 4 5 6 7

52. Employing effective problem solving and conflict resolution strategies.   1 2 3 4 5 6 7

53. Demonstrating effective decision-making skills.   1 2 3 4 5 6 7

54. Conducting effective meetings.   1 2 3 4 5 6 7

> *STANDARD THREE: The effective principal facilitates the development and maintenance of organizational and managerial systems consistent with the vision of the school community.*

PERFORMANCE COMPETENCIES

55. Managing change.   1 2 3 4 5 6 7

56. Ensuring that all personnel understand their roles in the organization.   1 2 3 4 5 6 7

57. Creating conditions that motivate.   1 2 3 4 5 6 7

58. Empowering others by delegating responsibility.   1 2 3 4 5 6 7

59. Developing strategic plans and organizational structures to support the implementation of the school's mission.   1 2 3 4 5 6 7

60. Bringing the various systems of the school into a cohesive plan that supports the school mission.   1 2 3 4 5 6 7

61. Working closely with managers of important systems within the school (e.g., custodial area) and the school system.   1 2 3 4 5 6 7

62. Developing a comprehensive plan for and monitoring and assessing the impact of organizational systems on the mission of the school.   1 2 3 4 5 6 7

63. Monitoring personnel responsible for all systems.   1 2 3 4 5 6 7

64. Eliminating unnecessary system functions.   1 2 3 4 5 6 7

65. Managing one's own time in a way that demonstrates commitment to the school mission.   1 2 3 4 5 6 7

66. Providing timely and useful data on organizational systems to supervisors and members of the school team.   1 2 3 4 5 6 7

67. Meeting deadlines in carrying out responsibilities.   1 2 3 4 5 6 7

68. Managing facilities that project an image of pride to students, families, and the community.   1 2 3 4 5 6 7

69. Maintaining accurate financial records.   1 2 3 4 5 6 7

70. Ensuring that needed technological support is in place.   1 2 3 4 5 6 7

71. Ensuring the availability of support services for students (e.g., health service, co-curricular activities).   1 2 3 4 5 6 7

72. Processing paperwork effectively and quickly—not becoming enmeshed in paperwork or allowing it to detract energy from achieving the school mission.   1 2 3 4 5 6 7

> *STANDARD FOUR: The effective principal exhibits team building skills in the development of ownership among all stakeholders in the school community.*

PERFORMANCE COMPETENCIES

73. Analyzing and interpreting the larger community in which the school is nested.   1 2 3 4 5 6 7

74. Studying and incorporating community values, standards, and culture into school decisions. 1 2 3 4 5 6 7

75. Utilizing the community as a resource for learning. 1 2 3 4 5 6 7

76. Helping the school participate in community development and community affairs. 1 2 3 4 5 6 7

77. Being highly visible in the external school community and being accessible to parents and other community members. 1 2 3 4 5 6 7

78. Maintaining open channels of communication and communicating with the external school community. 1 2 3 4 5 6 7

79. Communicating effectively with the media. 1 2 3 4 5 6 7

80. Developing and implementing strategies to involve parents and other community members in the life of the school. 1 2 3 4 5 6 7

81. Soliciting input from stakeholders. 1 2 3 4 5 6 7

82. Using knowledge, competencies, and experiences of stakeholders in the service of school goals. 1 2 3 4 5 6 7

83. Making stakeholders feel important to the organization. 1 2 3 4 5 6 7

84. Recognizing and rewarding contributions from stakeholders. 1 2 3 4 5 6 7

85. Helping others see the results of their input and work. 1 2 3 4 5 6 7

86. Promoting ownership. 1 2 3 4 5 6 7

87. Clarifying the agendas and responsibilities of stakeholders. 1 2 3 4 5 6 7

88. Establishing parameters for stakeholders. 1 2 3 4 5 6 7

89. Building partnerships and coalitions with key community groups and agencies. 1 2 3 4 5 6 7

90. Demonstrating the range of skills needed for team building and coalition building. 1 2 3 4 5 6 7

91. Demonstrating persistence in keeping groups focused and active in their commitment to the school. 1 2 3 4 5 6 7

92. Building trust among community partners and between the school and its partners. 1 2 3 4 5 6 7

93. Promoting the development of leadership within the team. 1 2 3 4 5 6 7

94. Using coaching techniques to help team members achieve their goals. 1 2 3 4 5 6 7

95. Coordinating resources of various partners to help the school achieve its mission. 1 2 3 4 5 6 7

96. Sorting out and helping individuals and groups assess their objectives while achieving common goals. 1 2 3 4 5 6 7

> *STANDARD FIVE: The effective principal models and promotes ethics and integrity in professional and personal activities.*

PERFORMANCE COMPETENCIES

97. Demonstrating genuine concern and respect for parents, faculty/staff, and students. 1 2 3 4 5 6 7

98. Treating others with dignity and sensitivity. 1 2 3 4 5 6 7

99. Exhibiting high moral standards. 1 2 3 4 5 6 7

100. Modeling principle-centered leadership. 1 2 3 4 5 6 7

101. Ensuring that the important educational and moral values of the school community influence decisions. 1 2 3 4 5 6 7

102. Doing what he/she says he/she will do. 1 2 3 4 5 6 7

103. Demonstrating courage in decision making. 1 2 3 4 5 6 7

104. Applying policies and procedures in a fair (equitable) and impartial manner. 1 2 3 4 5 6 7

105. Performing duties in a non-arbitrary, non-manipulative, and non-capricious manner. 1 2 3 4 5 6 7

106. Avoiding using position for personal gain. 1 2 3 4 5 6 7

107. Developing a written code of ethics for the school. 1 2 3 4 5 6 7

108. Promoting ethical behavior throughout the school community; ensuring unethical behavior is dealt with. 1 2 3 4 5 6 7

109. Maintaining confidentiality of information. 1 2 3 4 5 6 7

110. Adhering to laws, policies, and regulations. 1 2 3 4 5 6 7

111. Evaluating personnel with regard to actual performance rather than hearsay or feelings. 1 2 3 4 5 6 7

112. Shepherding and maintaining public resources—acting in a fiscally responsible manner. 1 2 3 4 5 6 7

113. Making decisions on sound principles, values, data, policy, and law. 1 2 3 4 5 6 7

114. Supporting collaborative agreements. 1 2 3 4 5 6 7

115. Making ethics part of staff development activities. 1 2 3 4 5 6 7

**CORWIN
PRESS**

The Corwin Press logo—a raven striding across an open book—represents the union of courage and learning. Corwin Press is committed to improving education for all learners by publishing books and other professional development resources for those serving the field of PreK–12 education. By providing practical, hands-on materials, Corwin Press continues to carry out the promise of its motto: **"Helping Educators Do Their Work Better."**

NATIONAL ASSOCIATION OF ELEMENTARY SCHOOL PRINCIPALS
Serving All Elementary and Middle Level Principals

Serving All Elementary and Middle Level Principals

The 29,500 members of the National Association of Elementary School Principals provide administrative and instructional leadership for public and private elementary and middle schools throughout the United States, Canada, and overseas. Founded in 1921, NAESP is today a vigorously independent professional association with its own headquarters building in Alexandria, Virginia, just across the Potomac River from the nation's capital. From this special vantage point, NAESP conveys the unique perspective of the elementary and middle school principal to the highest policy councils of our national government. Through national and regional meetings, award-winning publications, and joint efforts with its 50 state affiliates, NAESP is a strong advocate both for its members and for the 33 million American children enrolled in preschool, kindergarten, and grades 1 through 8.

**NATIONAL ASSOCIATION
OF SECONDARY SCHOOL
PRINCIPALS**

Promoting Excellence in School Leadership

The National Association of Secondary School Principals—promoting excellence in school leadership since 1916—provides its members the professional resources to serve as visionary leaders. NASSP further promotes student leadership development through its sponsorship of the National Honor Society®, the National Junior Honor Society®, and the National Association of Student Councils®. For more information visit, www.principals.org.